T0247798

Performance Management and Assessment of Federally Funded Research and Development Centers

Lessons from Academic Literature and Practitioner Guidance

VICTORIA A. GREENFIELD, SANDRA KAY EVANS, LAURA WERBER, SAMANTHA CHERNEY, LISA PELLED COLABELLA

Prepared for the Department of the Air Force
Approved for public release; distribution unlimited

PROJECT AIR FORCE

For more information on this publication, visit **www.rand.org/t/RRA737-2**.

About RAND

The RAND Corporation is a research organization that develops solutions to public policy challenges to help make communities throughout the world safer and more secure, healthier and more prosperous. RAND is nonprofit, nonpartisan, and committed to the public interest. To learn more about RAND, visit www.rand.org.

Research Integrity

Our mission to help improve policy and decisionmaking through research and analysis is enabled through our core values of quality and objectivity and our unwavering commitment to the highest level of integrity and ethical behavior. To help ensure our research and analysis are rigorous, objective, and nonpartisan, we subject our research publications to a robust and exacting quality-assurance process; avoid both the appearance and reality of financial and other conflicts of interest through staff training, project screening, and a policy of mandatory disclosure; and pursue transparency in our research engagements through our commitment to the open publication of our research findings and recommendations, disclosure of the source of funding of published research, and policies to ensure intellectual independence. For more information, visit www.rand.org/about/principles.

RAND's publications do not necessarily reflect the opinions of its research clients and sponsors.

Published by the RAND Corporation, Santa Monica, Calif.
© 2022 RAND Corporation
RAND® is a registered trademark.

Library of Congress Cataloging-in-Publication Data is available for this publication.

ISBN: 978-1-9774-0732-0

Cover: photo by Funtap/Adobe Stock.

About This Report

Many U.S. government agencies rely on federally funded research and development centers (FFRDCs) for independent expertise in systems engineering and integration, study and analysis, and research and development. In this report, we discuss insights from academic literature and practitioner guidance on the effective oversight, management, and performance assessment of FFRDCs. This research was conducted as part of a larger RAND Project AIR FORCE project to help the U.S. Air Force Space and Missile Command (SMC) strengthen processes for assessing the performance of its systems engineering and integration FFRDCs. However, the insights from literature discussed in this report should be of interest to other federal agencies seeking to improve their processes for assessing FFRDCs.

The research reported here was commissioned by SMC and conducted within the Resource Management Program of RAND Project AIR FORCE as part of a fiscal year 2019 project Performance Assessment Process Improvement for System Engineering Support to the Space and Missile Systems Center.

RAND Project AIR FORCE

RAND Project AIR FORCE (PAF), a division of the RAND Corporation, is the Department of the Air Force's (DAF's) federally funded research and development center for studies and analyses, supporting both the United States Air Force and the United States Space Force. PAF provides DAF with independent analyses of policy alternatives affecting the development, employment, combat readiness, and support of current and future air, space, and cyber forces. Research is conducted in four programs: Strategy and Doctrine; Force Modernization and Employment; Manpower, Personnel, and Training; and Resource Management. The research reported here was prepared under contract FA7014-16-D-1000.

Additional information about PAF is available on our website:
www.rand.org/paf/

This report documents work originally shared with DAF on April 25, 2019. The draft report, issued on May 31, 2019, was reviewed by formal peer reviewers and DAF subject-matter experts.

Contents

Figures

Tables

Summary

Many U.S. government agencies rely on nonprofit federally funded research and development centers (FFRDCs) for independent expertise in systems engineering and integration (SE&I), study and analysis, and research and development. The relationship between a sponsor at a government agency and an FFRDC differs from that of an ordinary commercial contracting relationship not just because of the FFRDC's not-for-profit status but also because of the relationship's intended longevity and reliance on trust.

In this report, we discuss insights drawn from academic literature and practitioner guidance that are applicable to the government's effective oversight, management, and performance assessment of FFRDCs. The research was conducted as part of a larger RAND Project AIR FORCE project to help the U.S. Air Force Space and Missile Command strengthen processes for assessing the performance of its SE&I FFRDCs, but it has broader implications for other sponsors of FFRDC-type relationships

We draw from best practices found in academic literature and practitioners' guidance to identify (1) institutional prerequisites for enabling effective oversight, management, and performance assessment of FFRDCs and (2) operational criteria for running constructive assessment processes. Such prerequisites encompass the systems, processes, doctrine, culture, and other institutional infrastructure without which oversight, management, and assessment cannot occur effectively, regardless of the inherent qualities of each.

Absent a substantial literature on sponsor engagement with FFRDCs, we turned to work on performance management (PM) systems and related or subsidiary processes, including performance assessments and program evaluation, which applies broadly to such engagement. For example, the literature on PM systems suggests that a PM system should fit an organization's mission, structure, culture, and values and draw from and feed into various strategic, administrative, and other institutional processes. To accomplish the latter, it should, on the one hand, use an organization's goals to gauge performance and, on the other hand, generate performance data that can be used to inform strategy development, planning for future needs, and resource allocation decisions (see Figure S.1 and Chapter 2).

Figure S.1. Performance Management System "Shoulds" and Institutional Prerequisites

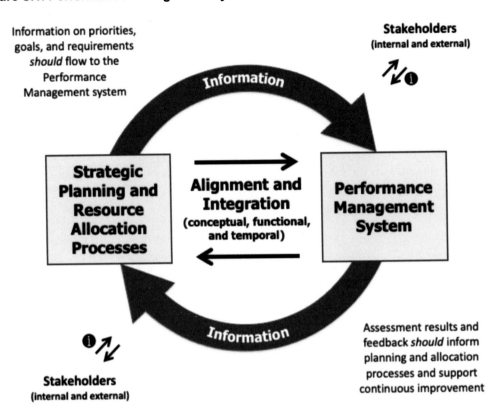

NOTE: Strategic planning and resource allocation processes include capability-planning and goal-setting.

These "shoulds," in turn, suggest a small set of institutional prerequisites for effective oversight, management, and performance assessment of FFRDCs, consisting of (1) a strategy that articulates the organization's priorities and goals, (2) planning, resource allocation, and other decisionmaking processes for supporting and implementing the organization's strategy, (3) alignment and integration among the organization's processes and systems, and (4) mechanisms for reaching out to and communicating with stakeholders (see Chapter 2).

The literature also points to a much a larger set of operational criteria needed to run a constructive assessment process, which includes the following: (1) the purpose and scope of the assessment are clear, widely disseminated, and shared by stakeholders and meet strategic and administrative needs, (2) grading factors address an organization's underlying priorities, goals, and concerns, (3) grading standards are applied consistently and are unbiased, without a propensity toward low or high grading, (4) sources of evidence provide information from which to draw necessary and sufficient evidence, (5) unintended consequences are assessed and mitigated or treated, (6) deliverables and timelines meet compliance needs and dovetail with other institutional processes, (7) training imparts knowledge and skills and can yield stakeholder buy-in, (8) pilot testing occurs before launching a full-scale assessment and with significant process changes, and (9) process evaluation provides the means to regularly assess, improve, and update the assessment process, including through stakeholder feedback (see Chapter 3).

Acknowledgments

For this project, we had an exceptionally close working relationship with our sponsor and the personnel at Space and Missile Systems Center (SMC). We thank Lt Gen John F. Thompson at SMC, who took a personal interest in this study throughout its execution. Within SMC's Program Management and Integration office, Cordell DeLaPena provided constructive, valuable feedback on our analysis throughout the course of the project. Mark Scatolini worked with us on an ongoing basis as our principal point of contact, facilitating the successful completion of our project through a variety of means.

We also benefited from the contributions of our RAND colleagues. Anita Szafran provided thorough searches as part of our efforts to locate literature on performance management and related concepts, Kristin Leuschner contributed to developing visual displays and summary materials for project deliverables, Holly Johnson worked with us on document preparation, and Robert Guffey crafted text and tables for the final product. Obaid Younossi and Ted Harshberger offered sound advice throughout the project as Director of RAND Project Air Force's Resource Management Program and Vice President and Director of RAND Project Air Force, respectively. Catherine Augustine and Shirley Ross provided careful, detailed peer reviews that strengthened the final product considerably.

We thank them all but retain full responsibility for the objectivity, accuracy, and analytic integrity of the work presented here.

Abbreviations

CPARS	Contractor Performance Assessment Reporting System
DoD	U.S. Department of Defense
DoDI	Department of Defense Instruction
DOE	U.S. Department of Energy
FAR	Federal Acquisition Regulation
FFRDC	federally funded research and development center
GAO	U.S. Government Accountability Office
GPRA	Government Performance and Results Act
JPL	Jet Propulsion Laboratory
M&O	management and operations
NASA	National Aeronautics and Space Administration
NIOSH	National Institute for Occupational Safety and Health
PART	Program Assessment Rating Tool
PEMP	Performance Evaluation and Management Plan
PM	performance management
S&T	science and technology
SE&I	systems engineering and integration
SMC	Space and Missile Systems Center

1. Background

Many U.S. government agencies rely on nonprofit federally funded research and development centers (FFRDCs) for independent expertise in systems engineering and integration (SE&I), study and analysis, and research and development. The relationship between a sponsor at a government agency and an FFRDC differs from that of an ordinary commercial contracting relationship not just because of the FFRDC's not-for-profit status but also because of the relationship's intended longevity and reliance on trust. Under Federal Acquisition Regulation (FAR) 35.017(a)(2),

> An FFRDC meets some special long-term research or development need which cannot be met as effectively by existing in-house or contractor resources. FFRDC's enable agencies to use private sector resources to accomplish tasks that are integral to the mission and operation of the sponsoring agency. An FFRDC, in order to discharge its responsibilities to the sponsoring agency, has access, beyond that which is common to the normal contractual relationship, to Government and supplier data, including sensitive and proprietary data, and to employees and installations equipment and real property. The FFRDC is required to conduct its business in a manner befitting its special relationship with the Government, to operate in the public interest with objectivity and independence, to be free from organizational conflicts of interest, and to have full disclosure of its affairs to the sponsoring agency[1]

In this report, we discuss insights drawn from academic literature and practitioner guidance that are applicable to the effective oversight, management, and performance assessment of FFRDCs.[2] The research was conducted as part of a larger RAND Project AIR FORCE project to help the U.S. Air Force Space and Missile Command (SMC) strengthen processes for assessing the performance of its SE&I FFRDCs, but it has broader implications for other sponsors of FFRDC-type relationships.[3]

We draw from best practices found in academic literature and practitioners' guidance to identify (1) institutional prerequisites for enabling effective oversight, management, and performance assessment of FFRDCs and (2) operational criteria for running constructive assessment processes.[4] Such prerequisites encompass the systems, processes, doctrine, culture,

---

[1] In addition, federal law authorizes agencies to contract with FFRDCs on a sole-source basis. See 10 U.S.C. § 2304(b)(1)(C).

[2] In this literature review, we tend to use the terms *performance assessment* and *performance assessment process*, but we also use related terms (referring, for example, to *reviews*, *appraisals*, etc.).

[3] For example, some insights might be relevant to relationships with University Affiliated Research Centers.

[4] The Defense Acquisition University defines a *best practice* as something that

> has been generally accepted for producing results that are superior to those achieved by other means or because it has become a standard way of doing things—e.g., of complying with legal or

and other institutional infrastructure without which oversight, management, and assessment cannot occur effectively, regardless of the inherent qualities of each. Whereas academics and practitioners have written volumes on *internal assessment*—when an organization examines its own programs and employees—and commercial acquisitions, they have had comparatively little to say about relationships involving FFRDCs.[5] Consequently, no single body of academic research or practitioner guidance—or case comparison—matches the circumstances of those relationships directly or comprehensively.

However, much of our interest in government oversight of and engagement with FFRDCs falls within the boundaries of research on performance management (PM) systems and related or subsidiary processes, including performance assessments and program evaluation.[6] Organizations use PM systems, which tend to take a broad, systemic approach to monitoring and assessments, to develop "outcome-oriented goals and performance targets, monitor progress, stimulate performance improvements, and communicate results to higher policy levels and the public."[7] Among other functions, they represent the range of practices that an organization uses to produce "performance information through strategic planning and performance measurement routines" to inform decisionmaking.[8] Program evaluation, which tends to have a more targeted focus on the effectiveness of a particular program, involves "the application of systematic methods to address questions about program operations and results. It may include ongoing monitoring of a program as well as one-shot studies of program processes or program impact."[9]

Thus, we examine a wide range of literature and guidance on PM and program evaluation, looking for best practices in other potentially analogous and relevant organizational contexts (see Box 1.1). Insomuch as we can identify institutional prerequisites for effective PM systems and operational criteria for running effective assessment processes in those contexts, we can attempt

---

ethical requirements. Best practices are used to maintain quality as an alternative to mandatory legislated standards and can be based on self-assessment or benchmarking (Craig M. Arndt, "Using Industry Best Practices to Improve Acquisition," Defense Acquisition University, June 20, 2018).

[5] The literature also speaks to *external*, or third-party, assessment. See, e.g., Institute of Medicine and National Research Council, *Hearing Loss Research at NIOSH: Reviews of Research Programs of the National Institute for Occupational Safety and Health*, Washington, D.C.: National Academies Press, August 29, 2006; and National Research Council, *The Measure of STAR: Review of the U.S. Environmental Protection Agency's Science to Achieve Results (STAR) Research Grants Program*, Washington, D.C.: National Academies Press, 2003.

[6] The PM system literature does not cover all areas of interest to this project: e.g., it does not address contracting, legal, and regulatory matters, nor does it address the mechanics of allocating technical effort specifically.

[7] Joseph S. Wholey, "Use of Evaluation in Government: The Politics of Evaluation," in Joseph S. Wholey, Harry P. Hatry, and Kathryn E. Newcomer, eds., *Handbook of Practical Program Evaluation*, 3rd ed., San Francisco, Calif.: Jossey-Bass, 2010, pp. 653–654.

[8] Donald P. Moynihan, *The Dynamics of Performance Management: Constructing Information and Reform*, Washington, D.C.: Georgetown University Press, 2008.

[9] Kathryn E. Newcomer, Harry P. Hatry, and Joseph S. Wholey, "Planning and Designing Useful Evaluations," in Wholey, Hatry, and Newcomer, 2010, pp. 5–6.

to single out prerequisites and criteria in this context. In essence, getting the PM system "right" would mean getting many of the relevant oversight, management, and assessment parameters right. The fit and application might not be perfect, but we can modify and supplement as needed to account for contextual differences and other needs.[10]

Box 1.1. Literature Search Methods and Parameters

To support this research effort, we conducted an integrated literature review in which we synthesized materials about PM, including PM systems, program evaluation, and related policy matters, looking for best practices in other potentially analogous and relevant organizational contexts.[a]

We used variations of keywords related to PM, program evaluation, contractors, and FFRDCs to search several leading research databases. More specifically, we searched the EBSCO databases: Academic Search Complete, Business Book Summaries, Business Source Complete, eBook Business Collection, Military and Government Collection, and Social Sciences Abstracts. Our search strategy focused on different combinations and variations of terms, including evaluate, appraise, assess, measure, perform, contractors, professional services, and FFRDC. For example, we searched the EBSCO databases on

- (evaluat* OR apprais* OR assess* OR measur*) N5 (perform* OR FFRDC OR "professional services")
- ((evaluat* OR apprais* OR assess* OR measur*) N5 perform*) AND (contractors OR "professional services" OR ffrdc OR "federally funded research and development centers"),

where N5 means within five words of each other.

In addition, we followed leads from those searches (e.g., in citations and references in books or articles) to uncover related research, and we reviewed U.S. Government Accountability Office (GAO) reports on FFRDC oversight, federal guidance on oversight, previous RAND research, and practitioner-produced content on PM systems and program evaluation, among other sources (including some from our archives). Because the literature connected to these areas is so vast, we sought out key references, such as highly cited academic texts, practitioner resources, and policy guidance.

Given the context of SMC's oversight of and engagement with the SE&I FFRDCs (e.g., the contractual principle of privity, which limits a sponsor's direct involvement with an FFRDC's employees), we do not lean heavily on the literatures on employee accountability or employee-level performance appraisal practices but rather try to draw organizational analogies where possible and constructive. Although employee accountability and appraisal are important parts of PM, they were not a focus of the larger project for SMC because we were not tasked with examining how SMC appraises or evaluates SMC personnel and because SMC cannot appraise or evaluate SE&I FFRDC personnel for the aforementioned reasons of privity.

Even with this relatively narrow set of parameters, our search yielded a large body of articles, books, and reports that we synthesized to identify best practices for SE&I FFRDC PM.

[a] Richard J. Torraco, "Writing Integrative Literature Reviews: Using the Past and Present to Explore the Future," *Human Resource Development Review*, Vol. 15, No. 4, December 2016.

Among the salient sources of insight to public-sector management, we draw from work that emerged alongside federal agencies' efforts to satisfy provisions of the Government Performance and Results Act (GPRA) and implement the associated Program Assessment Rating Tool (PART).[11] The legislation, enacted in 1993 and revamped in 2010, and tool aimed to increase

---

[10] We do not lean heavily on the literature on employee accountability or employee-level performance appraisal practices. Although employee accountability and appraisal are important parts of PM, they are not a focus of this literature review because we are not examining how FFRDC sponsors engage with FFRDC personnel and because those sponsors cannot, contractually, appraise or evaluate an FFRDC's personnel.

[11] Victoria A. Greenfield, Valerie L. Williams, and Elisa Eiseman, *Using Logic Models for Strategic Planning and Evaluation: Application to the National Center for Injury Prevention and Control*, Santa Monica, Calif.: RAND

accountability in government agencies by linking funding to performance and requiring agencies to develop and regularly update multiyear strategic plans,[12] as well as annual plans, to assess performance measures related to program outputs, outcomes, and services.[13] GPRA and PART have been subjects of criticism (e.g., for being burdensome),[14] but GPRA, PART, and the literature they inspired speak to agencies' needs for underlying institutional infrastructure and robust methods of assessment.

The literature, overall, has much to say about what to do and what not to do institutionally and operationally, either by implication or explicitly. In the chapters that follow, we start with the positive, with observations from the literature that suggest promising practices for oversight, management, assessment, institutional prerequisites, operational criteria, and paths forward. In some instances, the literature suggests an obvious prerequisite or criteria; in others, we must work to back it out from a related "should." To illustrate, one author indicates that effective PM systems should support organizational performance by linking goal-setting, performance measures, and reward systems in ways that support desired outcomes such as impact or innovation.[15] This "should" implies certain institutional "must haves," including aligned and integrated institutional processes, well-articulated goals, and an awareness and understanding of desired outcomes and impact. Lastly, we turn to the negative, with observations on symptoms of failure. These symptoms can also provide red flags when assessing how an FFRDC sponsor is performing in its "as-is" state in relation to best practices.

In Chapter 2, we identify prerequisites for effective PM. In Chapter 3, we examine criteria for an effective performance assessment process. Finally, we address potential weaknesses in program management systems and assessment processes in Chapter 4. In each chapter, we summarize the lessons from academic literature and practitioner guidance and discuss how they apply to overseeing, managing, and assessing FFRDCs.

Corporation, TR-370-NCIPC, 2006; and Valerie L. Williams, Elisa Eiseman, Eric Landree, and David M. Adamson, *Demonstrating and Communicating Research Impact: Preparing NIOSH Programs for External Review*, Santa Monica, Calif.: RAND Corporation, MG-809-NIOSH, 2009.

[12] Herman Aguinis, "An Expanded View of Performance Management," in James W. Smither and Manuel London, eds., *Performance Management: Putting Research into Action*, San Francisco, Calif.: Jossey-Bass, 2009.

[13] Alan W. Steiss, *Strategic Management for Public and Nonprofit Organizations*, New York: Marcel Dekker, 2003. The 2010 modernization of the GPRA further required agencies to establish goals, hold personnel accountable for goal achievement, and conduct quarterly progress reviews (U.S. Government Accountability Office, "Performance Measurement and Evaluation: Definitions and Relationships," Washington, D.C., GAO-11-646SP, May 2011).

[14] Brian M. Stecher, Frank Camm, Cheryl L. Damberg, Laura S. Hamilton, Kathleen J. Mullen, Christopher Nelson, Paul Sorensen, Martin Wachs, Allison Yoh, Gail L. Zellman, and Kristin J. Leuschner, *Toward a Culture of Consequences: Performance-Based Accountability Systems for Public Services,* Santa Monica, Calif.: RAND Corporation, MG-1019, 2010.

[15] Moynihan, 2008.

2. Institutional Prerequisites for Effective Performance Management

In this chapter, we consider the literatures on PM systems and program evaluation to identify institutional prerequisites for effective oversight, management, and assessment of external support entities, including FFRDCs. By *prerequisites*, we mean the institutional infrastructure—e.g., systems, processes, doctrine, and culture—without which oversight, management, and assessment cannot occur effectively, regardless of the inherent qualities of each. For example, a performance assessment process could be well-designed in most or all regards, but, absent these prerequisites, it cannot serve its purpose.

Neither the PM systems nor program evaluation literature addresses institutional prerequisites head on, but together they provide an entry point for identifying or backing out prerequisites by characterizing institutional "shoulds" and "should nots" and addressing how agencies can most effectively manage their performance. These bodies of literature focus on different phenomena and differ in breadth, but they address similar cycles of information-gathering, feedback, and communication.[16]

The literature on PM systems suggests that an effective system should fit an organization's context and function holistically while serving the "core purposes" of PM, which are both strategic and administrative.[17] By *fitting the context of the organization*, we mean that the organization's overall approach to PM, including assessment, needs to be tailored to its distinct mission and structure, even if it draws fruitfully from other agencies' PM models. *Functioning holistically* means viewing PM at a "systems level" that extends beyond the PM system, in which the parts work together and form a coherent whole. Further, to both fit contextually and function holistically, a PM system should reflect an organization's values and culture, not just its concerns about cost or efficiency.[18] One author suggests that good PM systems "are not isolated systems" that operate in vacuums but are "highly integrated into the philosophy, values, and [other] systems of the organization."[19]

---

[16] Newcomer, Hatry, and Wholey, 2010; Peter H. Rossi, Howard E. Freeman, and Mark W. Lipsey, *Evaluation: A Systematic Approach*, 6th ed., Thousand Oaks, Calif.: SAGE Publications, 1999.

[17] Aguinis, 2009; Herman Aguinis, *Performance Management*, 3rd ed., Boston, Mass.: Pearson Education, 2013; and William A. Schiemann, "Aligning Performance Management with Organizational Strategy, Values, and Goals," in Smither and London, 2009.

[18] Kit Fai Pun and Anthony Sydney White, "A Performance Measurement Paradigm for Integrating Strategy Formulation: A Review of Systems and Frameworks," *International Journal of Management Reviews*, Vol. 7, No. 1, March 2005; and Schiemann, 2009.

[19] Schiemann, 2009, pp. 78–79. Among those values, the author cites accountability and transparency.

Furthermore, intended changes in a PM system should lead to an end state that is compatible with an organization's culture.[20] In a review of PM implementation studies, researchers found that organizational culture was the third-most-frequently cited implementation factor, trailing only leadership commitment and support and the designed quality of the PM system.[21] The literature further suggests that if the values and beliefs underpinning an organization's culture are inconsistent with intended changes in its PM system, the changes may not stick without persistent intervention.[22]

Taken together, these perspectives on PM systems suggest three interrelated areas of "shoulds," which we address in turn: (1) strategic alignment and integration, (2) decisionmaking, and (3) feedback, improvement, and communication.

Strategic Alignment and Integration

The literature describes deep and far-reaching connections between PM and strategy, in terms of both development and implementation.[23] In a public sector context, PM systems should gather performance data that are connected with progress toward goals; communicate data to employees and other stakeholders (including the public) and obtain their feedback; use the data and feedback for strategic planning, including goal-setting processes; and then repeat.[24]

In effect, a PM system should draw from and feed into various strategic and other institutional processes. For example, a PM system should, on the one hand, use an organization's goals to gauge—or develop gauges for—performance and, on the other hand, generate performance data that that can be used to inform strategy development, planning for future needs, and resource allocation decisions.

The "cyclicality" of PM means that not only should a PM system serve a strategic purpose, it should also be integrated into and coordinated with an organization's strategic planning process.

---

[20] Judith A. Neal and Cheryl L. Tromley, "From Incremental Change to Retrofit: Creating High-Performance Work Systems," *Academy of Management Executive*, Vol. 9, No. 1, February 1995.

[21] Heather Keathley-Herring and Eileen M. Van Aken, "Systematic Literature Review on the Factors That Affect Performance Measurement System Implementation," *Proceedings of the 2013 Industrial and Systems Engineering Research Conference*, 2013.

[22] Neal and Tromley, 1995.

[23] Aguinis, 2009; Pun and White, 2005. Strategic planning is a deliberative, disciplined approach to producing fundamental decisions and actions that shape and guide what an organization is, what it does, and why it does it, by creating formal and informal forums in which important issues can be identified and addressed, useful learning can occur, and results can be carried forward toward wise divisions in relevant areas. See Donald P. Moynihan and Noel Landuyt, "How Do Public Organizations Learn? Bridging Cultural and Structural Perspectives," *Public Administration Review*, Vol. 69, No. 6, November–December 2009.

[24] Moynihan, 2008.

In short, an organization develops, implements, and revisits its strategic plan largely through the use of its PM system.[25]

Figure 2.1 captures elements of the connections to strategy and operations and, by extension, the embedded and nested nature of PM systems.[26]

Figure 2.1. Nested and Interlinked Processes and Operations

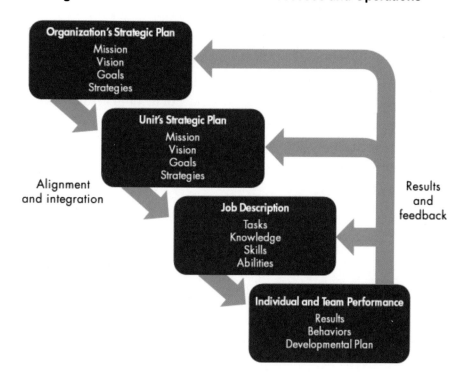

SOURCE: Adapted from Aguinis, 2013, p. 64, with authors' addition of results and feedback.

Goal-setting, which occurs under the auspices of strategic planning, should set the stage for strategy implementation and follow through and factor into the design and application of PM systems. As depicted by the downward flow in Figure 2.1, a PM system should be able to engage with and support an organization's strategy by mapping to and linking organizational goals with unit-level (e.g., division or program) or individual goals and by reinforcing consistent practices and behaviors at each level.[27] Some authors also suggest tying feedback on performance to organizational operations, not just unit-level operations, to show employees—and potentially others—how their work fits in with the larger whole.[28]

Goals can serve different purposes at different levels of the organization, including

---

[25] Aguinis, 2013.

[26] Aguinis, 2013, p. 64.

[27] Aguinis, 2009; Pun and White, 2005.

[28] Stanley B. Silverman and Wendy M. Muller, "Assessing Performance Management Programs and Policies," in Smither and London, 2009.

- defining intended accomplishments over a given time frame
- providing information about and for mission implementation
- acting as motivational targets for groups, employees, and, in the case of an FFRDC sponsor, the FFRDC(s) with which it contracts for services.[29]

Goals across organizational levels can also provide a basis for making decisions about the types and amounts of resources to allocate to particular activities and for gauging the performance of those resources, which can provide insight for subsequent decisionmaking (as discussed in the following section). Well-constructed goals will derive from institutional priorities and mark a path from *inputs*—labor, infrastructure, etc.—to *outcomes*, thereby suggesting the appropriate use of resources en route, a point that we return to in Chapter 3.[30] Such goals can also be used to develop yardsticks to allow "for a comparison of what needs to be achieved versus what each unit, group, and individual is achieving."[31]

The literature on PM systems and program evaluation suggests a role for performance measures in both developing goals and making progress toward meeting them.[32] For example, performance measures may be necessary

> for setting goals and objectives, planning program activities to accomplish these goals, allocating resources to these programs, monitoring and evaluating the results to determine if they are making progress in achieving the established goals and objectives, and modifying program plans to enhance performance.[33]

Box 2.1 describes a well-known approach to goal-setting and some alternatives.

---

[29] These purposes draw from Aguinis, 2013, p. 73, with some modification.

[30] Greenfield, Williams, and Eiseman, 2006; see also Figure 3.1 in this report and the related discussion of logic models in Chapter 3.

[31] Aguinis, 2013, p. 73.

[32] We discuss performance measures later in this report.

[33] Harry P. Hatry, James R. Fountain, Jr., Jonathan M. Sullivan, and Lorraine Kremer, eds., *Service Efforts and Accomplishments Reporting: Its Time Has Come: An Overview*, Norwalk, Conn.: Governmental Accounting Standards Board of the Financial Accounting Federation, 1990, p. v, as cited in Robert D. Behn, "Why Measure Performance? Different Purposes Require Different Measures," *Public Administration Review*, Vol. 63, No. 5, September 2003.

Box 2.1. Goal-Setting in Practice

As a practical matter, an organization's goals should be as simple as possible and can be set with help from standard approaches to goal-setting that address various aspects of the process. The use of SMART (Specific, Measurable, Attainable, Relevant, and Time-bound) goals is one example of a well-established approach to spelling out goals.[a] With program-level outcomes in mind, one set of researchers define SMART goals as follows:

- *Specific*. Describe precisely what is expected to change and for whom.
- *Measurable*. There must be a way to determine the presence or extent of change.
- *Achievable*. Outcomes must be feasible for the target population (e.g., based on prior empirical expectations for change).
- *Realistic*. Outcomes should be able to be accomplished with the available resources.
- *Time-bound*. Describe the time frame in which the change is expected to occur.[b]

Notably, the SMART goal approach does not take into consideration how to set the goals, who sets goals, or whether the goals are worthwhile.[c] Researchers also suggest potential pitfalls. For example, in extremely dynamic, uncertain environments, it can be difficult to manage using specific time-based objectives.[d] Moreover, too much specificity can stifle innovation, resulting in incremental change rather than breakthroughs.[e]

Other goal-setting approaches, such as cascading goals, address worth to some extent.[f] The cascading goals approach calls for aligning goals vertically throughout an organization's hierarchy so that an employee's goals coordinate with the goals of their supervisor, their division, and so on. This helps to address the question of worth, but the approach has been criticized for its overreliance on top-down guidance.[g] Balanced scorecard methods and logic modeling also emphasize aligning organizational strategy with performance measures, targets or goals, and initiatives designed to meet those goals.[h] Taken together, these approaches suggest a need for PM systems to address both goal alignment and goal development.

[a] George T. Doran, "There's a S.M.A.R.T. Way to Write Management's Goals and Objectives," *Management Review*, Vol. 70, No. 11, November 1981; Schiemann, 2009, p. 78; and Kellie C. Liket and Karen Maas, "Nonprofit Organizational Effectiveness: Analysis of Best Practices," *Nonprofit and Voluntary Sector Quarterly*, Vol. 44, No. 2, April 2015.
[b] Joie D. Acosta, Rajeev Ramchand, Amariah Becker, Alexandria Felton, and Aaron Kofner, *RAND Suicide Prevention Program Evaluation Toolkit*, Santa Monica, Calif.: RAND Corporation, TL-111-OSD, 2013, p. 25.
[c] Dick Grote, "3 Popular Goal-Setting Techniques Managers Should Avoid," *Harvard Business Review*, January 2, 2017.
[d] Martin Reeves and Jack Fuller, "When SMART Goals Are Not So Smart," *MIT Sloan Management Review*, March 21, 2018.
[e] Charles W. Prather, "The Dumb Thing About SMART Goals for Innovation," *Research-Technology Management*, Vol. 48, No. 5, 2005.
[f] Laurie E. Paarlberg and James L. Perry, "Values Management: Aligning Employee Values and Organization Goals," *American Review of Public Administration*, Vol. 37, No. 4, December 2007; and Elaine D. Pulakos, *Performance Management: A Roadmap for Developing, Implementing and Evaluating Performance Management Systems*, Alexandria, Va.: SHRM Foundation, 2004; and Schiemann, 2009.
[g] Grote, 2017.
[h] Robert S. Kaplan and David P. Norton, "Using the Balanced Scorecard as a Strategic Management System," *Harvard Business Review*, Vol. 85, No. 7/8, July–August 2007.

Applications to Decisionmaking

As an operational matter, a PM system should convey an organization's priorities (as reflected in its goals) and provide information for a variety of purposes, many but not all of which tie into strategy development and implementation, including evaluation efforts.[34] Arguably, a PM system's role in performance assessment is among its most essential functions,[35]

---

[34] Aguinis, 2009.

[35] Pun and White, 2005.

but it can serve other roles, too, especially in decisionmaking and related "organizational maintenance."[36] One author suggests that the PM system should support decisionmaking by providing stakeholders with information about how units (e.g., divisions or programs) are performing,[37] how well they are meeting expectations (e.g., in relation to an organization's strategy and goals), and where they need to improve.[38] Information from these areas can be used not just to rate performance but also to assess future needs, make decisions about allocating or acquiring resources to fill those needs, and influence the behavior of the workforce.[39] In the case of resource allocation decisions, an FFRDC sponsor might, for example, look to its strategic goals for initial guidance on allocating technical effort on an FFRDC contract but might turn to performance data for subsequent guidance on gross adjustments and fine tuning. Ideally, an organization would gather and use performance data to make decisions about allocating resources that also align with its strategy and goals.

Feedback, Improvement, and Communication

The literature points to the importance of ongoing monitoring and suggests, more fundamentally, creating a "culture of feedback" to support performance improvements.[40] The term *culture of feedback*[41] refers to the degree to which feedback, both formal and informal, is ingrained in an organization's culture and, practically speaking, its operations.[42] Researchers suggest that the extent to which individuals seek, value, and use feedback depends partly on the "feedback environment," arguing that a strong feedback culture can lead individuals to "seek and receive feedback more often, deal with it mindfully, and use it to calibrate and adjust their behavior to improve performance," to the benefit of an organization.[43]

To that end, employee feedback should be specific (e.g., directed at the task level of operations) and *developmental*, meaning that it enables supervisors to coach stakeholders and

---

[36] Aguinis, 2009, p. 9.

[37] Aguinis, 2009.

[38] Broadly speaking, *performance* refers to "outputs or outcomes of activities" or, from a public sector standpoint, "the realization of public value." See Wouter Van Dooren, Geert Bouckaert, and John Halligan, *Performance Management in the Public Sector*, New York: Routledge, 2010, p. 17. We define and say more about *outputs* and *outcomes* in later sections of this report.

[39] For more on these points and a related discussion of "talent inventories," see Aguinis, 2009; Behn, 2003; and Pun and White, 2005.

[40] Schiemann, 2009; Silverman and Muller, 2009.

[41] Manuel London and James W. Smither, "Feedback Orientation, Feedback Culture, and the Longitudinal Performance Management Process," *Human Resource Management Review*, Vol. 12, No. 1, Spring 2002, p. 81; and Silverman and Muller, 2009. Some researchers, such as Silverman and Muller, 2009, use the term *feedback environment*.

[42] Silverman and Muller, 2009, pp. 534–535.

[43] London and Smither, 2002, pp. 86 and 97.

supports learning (by asking whether something is working) and continuous improvement at various organizational levels.[44] As noted earlier, tying feedback to daily operations can also show employees that what they do affects the functioning of the organization.[45] Insomuch as the sponsor-FFRDC relationship allows for formal or informal engagement on daily operations with FFRDC staff, the same could be said in that environment. One author suggests that organizations should be prepared to step in early with support or resources when problems emerge, suggesting the importance of timely institutional follow through.[46]

Researchers describe a virtuous cycle of feedback: "As more and more individuals in the organization have positive experiences with feedback (using the feedback to pursue and attain behavior change and valued goals), the organization's feedback culture will become stronger."[47] Top leaders can act as role models to pattern values and norms (including those pertaining to feedback), which might further promote acculturation.[48]

In theory, it could be possible to rate the strength of an organization's feedback environment. For example, on a 1 to 5 scale, a rating of 1 could mean that an organization has no consistent feedback processes; a rating of 3 could mean the organization has a feedback system, but it is not consistent across the organization; and a rating of 5 could mean the organization has a well-defined, consistent feedback system.[49]

Some commercial organizations are opting for less-formal feedback-driven processes in lieu of more-formal review processes (as we discuss in the following chapter).[50] Some authors caution that organizations often place too much emphasis on revamping formal assessment tools without taking steps to improve supervisor-subordinate communication:

> The combination of documented performance standards to support ratings, formal manager calibration, and training and training transfer strategies to improve manager employee relationships and communication will be optimal practices in many situations. This is because this combination provides managers and employees with straightforward tools that facilitate performance

---

[44] Aguinis, 2009; Pun and White, 2005; Silverman and Muller, 2009, p. 535; and Chiara Demartini, *Performance Management Systems: Design, Diagnosis and Use*, Heidelberg, Germany: Physica-Verlag, 2014.

[45] Silverman and Muller, 2009, pp. 534–535.

[46] Schiemann, 2009.

[47] London and Smither, 2002, p. 95.

[48] Schiemann, 2009.

[49] Silverman and Muller, 2009, p. 535, sets out this example with greater detail.

[50] Seymour Adler, Michael Campion, Alan Colquitt, Amy Grubb, Kevin Murphy, Rob Ollander-Krane, and Elaine D. Pulakos, "Getting Rid of Performance Ratings: Genius or Folly? A Debate," *Industrial and Organizational Psychology*, Vol. 9, No. 2, 2016; and Angelo S. DeNisi and Kevin R. Murphy, "Performance Appraisal and Performance Management: 100 Years of Progress?" *Journal of Applied Psychology*, Vol. 102, No. 3, 2017.

management, while training and reinforcing them to exhibit behaviors that are essential for effective performance management outcomes.[51]

Others describe how performance measures can be used to motivate staff or other stakeholders, promote—or explain, as communication devices—work to external audiences (the public, for example), and celebrate accomplishments.[52] In these regards, the PM system can serve as a mechanism for transparent communication with stakeholders, both internal and external to an organization, including FFRDCs.

Feedback is a term commonly used to describe supervisor-subordinate communication about work performance,[53] but it is also subject to broader interpretation and is a subset of an organization's broader communication environment.[54] By implication, if a PM system is to serve stakeholders by providing them with information about organizational priorities, expectations, and, of course, performance, it must support communication, not just in the abstract but concretely. Moreover, it is not enough to simply "broadcast" information; stakeholders must receive it and be able to use it. Thus, an organization must have means to package information and transfer it to stakeholders to enable use.[55]

Crosswalk from Best Practices to Institutional Prerequisites

We conclude this chapter with a crosswalk, leading from the best practices (or "shoulds") that emerged from the academic literature and practitioner guidance to a set of institutional prerequisites for effective oversight, management, and assessment. The crosswalk consists of a diagram (Figure 2.2) that (1) ties the PM system to an organization's strategic planning and resource allocation processes, (2) designates "shoulds" within and throughout the cycle, and (3) enables us to extract a small number of primary institutional prerequisites.

---

[51] Elaine D. Pulakos and Ryan S. O'Leary, "Why Is Performance Management Broken?" *Industrial and Organizational Psychology*, Vol. 4, No. 2, June 2011, p. 162.

[52] Pun and White, 2005.

[53] For example, Aguinis, Gottfredson, and Joo, 2012, defines *performance feedback* as

> information about an employee's past behaviors with respect to established standards of employee behaviors and results. The goals of performance feedback are to improve individual and team performance, as well as employee engagement, motivation, and job satisfaction (Herman Aguinis, Ryan K. Gottfredson, and Harry Joo, "Delivering Effective Performance Feedback: The Strengths-Based Approach," *Business Horizons*, Vol. 55, No. 2, March–April 2012, p. 105).

See also London and Smither, 2002.

[54] For broader interpretations, see, e.g., Greenfield, Williams, and Eiseman, 2006; Eric Landree, Hirokazu Miyake, and Victoria A. Greenfield, *Nanomaterial Safety in the Workplace: Pilot Project for Assessing the Impact of the NIOSH Nanotechnology Research Center*, Santa Monica, Calif.: RAND Corporation, RR-1108-NIOSH, 2015; and Williams et al., 2009.

[55] See, e.g., Greenfield, Williams, and Eiseman, 2006; Landree, Miyake, and Greenfield, 2015; and Williams et al., 2009.

Figure 2.2. Performance Management System "Shoulds" and Institutional Prerequisites

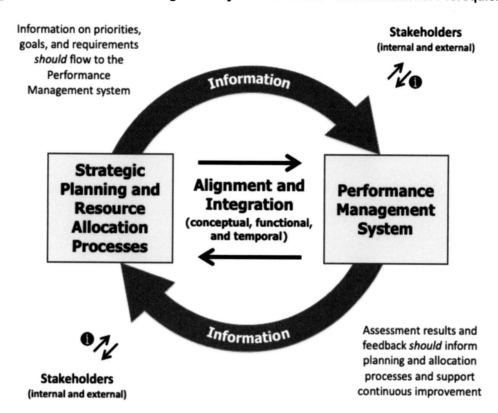

Information on priorities, goals, and requirements *should* flow to the Performance Management system

Stakeholders
(internal and external)

Information

Strategic Planning and Resource Allocation Processes

Alignment and Integration
(conceptual, functional, and temporal)

Performance Management System

Information

Stakeholders
(internal and external)

Assessment results and feedback *should* inform planning and allocation processes and support continuous improvement

NOTE: Strategic planning and resource allocation processes include capability-planning and goal-setting.

As shown in Figure 2.2, the PM system should align conceptually, functionally, and (less obviously) temporally with the organization's strategic planning and resource allocation processes, including those for goal-setting and capability-planning, while drawing from and feeding into those processes. On that basis, the PM system can convey priorities, support decisionmaking as it concerns strategic planning and resource allocation, and support development and continuous improvement. In regard to what one might call "pre-prerequisites," "alignment and integration" presume both the existence of a strategy that articulates the organization's priorities and goals and the processes to support and implement it, as well as mechanisms for communicating with stakeholders up, down, and across the organization and external to the organization. Regarding communication, the literature strongly suggests the merit of creating a "culture of feedback."

Thus, our primary institutional prerequisites consist of

- a strategy that articulates the organization's priorities and goals
- planning, resource allocation, and other decisionmaking processes for supporting and implementing the organization's strategy
- alignment and integration among the organization's processes and systems
- mechanisms for reaching out to and communicating with stakeholders.

In the next chapter, we dig into the content of the PM system, as shown on the right-hand side of Figure 2.2; specifically, we consider the characteristics of the assessment process and the criteria for an effective assessment process.

3. Operational Criteria for an Effective Performance Assessment Process

In this chapter, we turn to the academic literatures on PM systems and program evaluation and to practitioner guidance to identify best practices that point to criteria for developing an effective process to assess support from FFRDCs.[56] Whereas the previous chapter on institutional prerequisites addresses what an organization should do, at a high level, to support PM (including assessment), this chapter focuses on "shoulds" for conceptualizing, designing, and implementing formal assessments. We had to work to derive implied prerequisites in the previous chapter; in this chapter, however, the leap from "shoulds" to criteria tends to be more direct. In addition, we consider guidance on adherence to requirements for assessments—or "musts"—under provisions of the FAR and Department of Defense Instruction (DoDI) 5000.77 in effect at the time of our literature review.[57] FAR provisions apply to all federal agencies that work with FFRDCs, and DoDI 5000.77 provisions apply to U.S. Department of Defense (DoD) agencies.

We attempt to draw connections between the previous chapter and this chapter to identify higher-level "shoulds" that could affect the composition or functionality of the assessment process. For example, we relate broad findings on "strategic alignment and integration" in the previous chapter to detailed findings on "purpose and scope" in this chapter. Likewise, findings on the importance of accounting for organizational context track to more-granular findings on tailoring assessments. As one author says, "every evaluation must be tailored to the circumstances of the program being evaluated" to yield "credible and useful answers to the specific questions at issue while still being sufficiently practical to actually implement with the resources available."[58]

Lastly, the academic literature and practitioner guidance recognize that performance assessments require resources (e.g., staff time and managerial focus). Thus, one can—or "should"—also consider whether the proposed features of an assessment are efficacious, necessary, and sufficient. At the outset, this means asking such questions as whether a formal assessment is the best way to serve a given purpose, whether the scope of the assessment is broad enough or broader than it needs to be for that purpose, and whether a given feature of the assessment is the "right" feature in the "right" amount.

---

[56] Moreover, we do not address employee-level performance appraisal practices unless we can draw out a relevant organizational analogy.

[57] DoDI 5000.77, *DOD Federally Funded Research and Development Center (FFRDC) Program*, Washington, D.C.: U.S. Department of Defense, January 31, 2018.

[58] Rossi, Freeman, and Lipsey, 1999, p. 76.

We begin this chapter with process conceptualization, in the form of purpose and scope; then move on to design and implementation, with discussions of grading, evidence, stakeholder buy-in, and various technical concerns; and conclude with a summary table that lists each feature of the assessment process alongside criteria and related actions.

Purpose and Scope

Identifying the purpose—or "why?"—of a performance assessment is an important early step in planning because different purposes can call for different types of assessments, which cover different ground, possibly by different rules or procedures.[59]

According to one author, public-sector managers generally have one or more of the following eight reasons for measuring performance, most of which could apply to FFRDC sponsors:

- evaluating
- controlling behavior (e.g., ensuring the agency is doing what is needed)
- budgeting and resource allocation
- motivating
- promoting or presenting the organization to stakeholders (e.g., demonstrating that the agency is doing well)
- identifying and celebrating accomplishments
- learning (finding out what is or is not working)
- improving.[60]

Another author, also referring to public-sector settings, describes the purposes of program evaluation as improving performance, increasing transparency, and bolstering accountability.[61]

The provisions of the FAR and DoDI 5000.77 suggest another type of purpose: "compliance." The FAR and DoDI 5000.77 call for performance assessment, with different degrees of specificity and requirements, some of which we address in the following sections.

Similarly, whether addressing assessments of individuals, programs, suppliers, or other entities, practitioner guidance and related research highlight scoping as an important early step.[62] *Scope* refers to the "who, what, where, and when" of an evaluation: that is, who will be evaluated, what activities or job functions will be evaluated, the types of work that will be evaluated, and the location and time frame of the evaluation. Scoping establishes the basis for an evaluation, can help ensure that the breadth of the assessment is appropriate (e.g., that it does not

---

[59] Behn, 2003; Pulakos, 2004.

[60] Behn, 2003, p. 588.

[61] Wholey, 2010.

[62] Landree, Miyake, and Greenfield, 2015; IBM, *IBM Emptoris Supplier Lifecycle Management Performance Evaluation Guide*, Version 10.1.1, 2016; and U.S. Army Environmental Command, *Environmental Program Internal Assessment Guide*, Version 1.0, March 27, 2013.

overlook an important task or project or overreach), and provides clarity for evaluators, managers, staff, and other stakeholders.[63]

Although best practices on strategic alignment and integration suggest that the purpose and scope of the assessment "should" align with the priorities, goals, and concerns of the organization, regulatory and policy requirements imply that mere compliance constitutes a distinct "must."

For a compliance-oriented assessment, an organization, such as an FFRDC sponsor, might choose to focus on "mandatory" concerns as a bare minimum. For example, DoDI 5000.77 requires DoD agencies "to assess, at a minimum, technical quality, responsiveness, value, and timeliness" annually, and a compliance-oriented assessment might not exceed those bounds. By contrast, an assessment pegged to broader organizational priorities and concerns, which would be consistent with the best practices of the previous chapter, would necessarily reach farther and might do so at different or more frequent intervals. Moreover, an agency might take steps toward an integrative approach even when meeting the bare minimum in an assessment.

However, speaking to program evaluation, some authors warn that

> an evaluation can have breadth, depth, and rigor but will require proportionate funding and time. Or it can be cheap and quick but will, of necessity, either deal with a very narrow issue or be relatively superficial (or both).[64]

The same logic applies to performance assessment processes in general, and trying to do too much without enough resources can overburden staff and evaluators and lead to frustration, delays, and shoddy work.[65] Thus, an organization must be realistic about how much it can spend on assessment in relation to what it wants or needs to get from it.

Grading System

Next, we discuss what we term the *grading system*, delineating among *grading areas*, *grading factors*, and *grading standards*. This nomenclature draws from ideas in the academic literature and practitioner guidance, but it is not hard-and-fast. Rather, it represents a synthesis of approaches to sorting through various dimensions of grading, consisting of (1) categories of interest or inquiry, reflective of purpose and scope; (2) specific concerns about performance within each category that merit separate consideration and provide a basis for performance measurement; and (3) the standards by which organizations assign grades for each factor or area (e.g., "what is an A?"). By linking factors to measurement, we also call attention to performance measures, which we address in that context.

---

[63] Landree, Miyake, and Greenfield, 2015.

[64] Rossi, Freeman, and Lipsey, 1999, p. 54.

[65] Rossi, Freeman, and Lipsey, 1999, p. 54.

Ultimately, the literature and guidance, including reports from GAO,[66] suggest that grading areas, factors, and standards, by whatever name, should be clearly stated, communicated to stakeholders, and shared across stakeholders so that they can be implemented consistently, reliably, and unambiguously within and across assessments.[67] One researcher recommends using multiple indicators to help mitigate the potential for ambiguity, though GAO suggests that you can have too much of a good thing.[68]

Grading Areas

As a matter of practice, organizations (including federal agencies) tend to bundle concerns about performance in topical or functional *areas*, which they grade according to related *factors*.[69] For federal agencies, these areas must satisfy any regulatory or administrative requirements: e.g., by covering necessary ground in FAR 42.15 or DoDI 5000.77, as applicable. Moreover, these areas should address an agency's priorities, goals, concerns, etc., as expressed in purpose and scope, consistent with the pursuit of strategic alignment and integration. FAR 42.15 requires grades in six areas at a minimum to assess a contractor's performance, but it also allows grades for other areas of the agency's choosing;[70] DoDI 5000.77 requires the consideration of at least four similar areas to assess DoD-sponsored FFRDCs (see Table 3.1).[71] By allowing grading in other areas, the regulatory and policy language provides an opening for an agency to address issues of strategic importance that might fall outside the bounds of the basic requirements for "technical quality," among other areas. Nevertheless, threading the needle on the requirements under the FAR and DoDI 5000.77, if applicable—while addressing other priorities—might require some mapping.

---

[66] For example, GAO, *National Laboratories: DOE Needs to Improve Oversight of Work Performed for Non-DOE Entities*, Washington, D.C., GAO-14-78, October 2013; Andrew Neely, Chris Adams, and Mike Kennerley, *The Performance Prism: The Scorecard for Measuring and Managing Business Success*, London: Financial Times Prentice Hall, 2002; Stecher et al., 2010; and Robert S. Kaplan, "Strategic Performance Measurement and Management in Nonprofit Organizations," *Nonprofit Management & Leadership*, Vol. 11, No. 3, Spring 2001.

[67] Demartini, 2014; Craig Eric Schneier, Douglas G. Shaw, and Richard W. Beatty, "Performance Measurement and Management: A Tool for Strategy Execution," *Human Resource Management*, Vol. 30, No. 3, Fall 1991; Kaplan, 2001; Stecher et al., 2010.

[68] Robert C. Davis, *Selected International Best Practices in Police Performance Measurement*, Santa Monica, Calif.: RAND Corporation, TR-1153-MOI, 2012; and GAO, "NASA Procurement: Use of Award Fees for Achieving Program Outcomes Should Be Improved," Washington, D.C., GAO-07-58, January 2007.

[69] This is less a finding from literature or guidance and more a practical observation. An organization could create laundry lists of factors without bundling them topically or functionally, and, if it has just a few concerns, its "areas" and "factors" could be one and the same. That said, when bundling occurs along topical or functional lines that map to an organization's strategic goals and objectives, the approach dovetails with other best practices.

[70] The Contractor Performance Assessment Reporting System (CPARS) accommodates up to three other areas (CPARS, "Guidance for the Contractor Performance Assessment Reporting System (CPARS)," July 2018, p. 25).

[71] Note that FAR 42.15 refers to these areas as "factors," and related CPARS guidance calls them "evaluation areas" (CPARS, 2018, p. 25). We reserve the term *factors* for the elements—specific concerns—that comprise each area, which FAR 42.15 refers to as "sub factors."

Table 3.1. FAR 42.15 and DoDI 5000.77 Grading Areas

FAR 42.15 (at a minimum)	DoDI 5000.77 (at a minimum)
• Technical (quality of product or service)	• Technical quality
• Cost control	• Value
• Schedule/timeliness	• Timeliness
• Management or business relations	• Responsiveness
• Small business subcontracting	• —
• Regulatory compliance[a]	• —
• Other (as applicable)	• —

SOURCES: FAR 42.15 and DoDI 5000.77, 2018.
NOTES: FAR 42.15 and DoDI 5000.77 require annual assessments at a minimum.
[a] This area appears in guidance for the CPARS (CPARS, 2018, pp. 25 and 49). Under the FAR, an agency can report "not applicable" if it is not going to apply ratings to a particular area.

As an example of a goals-based approach to grading, the U.S. Department of Energy (DOE) specifies common, goals-based grading areas in its contracts with national laboratories in terms of science and technology (S&T), leadership and stewardship, and management and operations (M&O) goals.[72] Their goals do not—and need not—mimic the FAR areas, but they cover similar terrain.[73] For example, the three S&T goals for the laboratories are to (1) "Provide for Efficient and Effective Mission Accomplishment," (2) "Provide for Efficient and Effective Design Fabrication, Construction, and Operations of Research Facilities," and (3) "Provide for Efficient and Effective Science and Technology Program Management." DOE also defines each goal: for example, in the case of mission accomplishment,

> The science and technology programs at the Laboratory produce high-quality, original, and creative results that advance science and technology; demonstrate sustained scientific progress and impact; receive appropriate external recognition of accomplishments; and contribute to overall research and development goals of the Department and its customers.[74]

---

[72] DOE and Ames Laboratory, "Performance Evaluation Measurement Plan (PEMP), Applicable to the Operation of Ames Laboratory," Contract No. DE-AC02-07CH11358, 2018. DOE's oversight of its national laboratories has drawn substantial criticism over the years. Nevertheless, DOE's approach to assessment provides an example of one way to link grading areas to an organization's goals. For examples of recent reports on oversight, see, e.g., GAO, 2013; GAO, *Department of Energy: Performance Evaluations Could Better Assess Management and Operating Contractor Costs*, Washington, D.C., GAO-19-5, February 2019; and Venkatesh Narayanamurti, Laura Diaz Anadon, Gabriel Chan, and Amitai Y. Bin-Nun, "Securing America's Future: Realizing the Potential of the Department of Energy's National Laboratories," testimony presented before the Senate Appropriations Subcommittee on Energy and Water Development, Washington, D.C., October 28, 2015.
Although the goals—and objectives—are the same for all of the laboratories, the weighting can differ.

[73] These DOE contracts fall under different grading rules, but an agency could develop areas for management purposes and then "translate" them to satisfy regulatory requirements, assuming that they overlapped sufficiently; moreover, it can report "N/A" for an area if the area is not applicable.

[74] DOE and Ames Laboratory, 2018, p. 9.

DOE has adopted this approach in the Performance Evaluation and Management Plans (PEMPs) for a set of "performance-based" laboratory contracts, in which grades in each area tie to award fee and, in some instances, award-term extensions, but the organizing principle (i.e., a goal-based assessment) does not hinge on the contract structure.

The National Aeronautics and Space Administration (NASA) Jet Propulsion Laboratory's (JPL's) 2018 contract takes a similar tack, albeit with less "award" on the line, but it draws its goals directly from the FAR areas set out in this section.[75] For example, the first goal for assessment—for all NASA directorates and offices that participate in grading—is "Provide for Quality/Technical product or service and effective mission accomplishment."[76]

Grading Factors

Factors, in our parlance, represent specific concerns that, taken together, constitute a *grading area* and merit separate evaluation or measurement within each area. They represent a narrowing from the general to the particular as gradable focal points. (Others, as we discuss later, also refer to them as "subfactors.") One author, who focuses on program evaluation, argues for translating goals into measurable indicators of achievement and collecting information ("evidence") from relevant participants ("sources") but warns that this can be easier said than done.[77] The author notes that goals can be unclear, programs often serve many purposes, and it can be hard to determine which parts of a program are creating value.[78]

Drawing again from the DOE and NASA JPL examples, we see "grading areas" that correspond to "goals," as well as "grading factors" that correspond to "objectives" under each goal.[79] For example, DOE provides two objectives for the first S&T goal (mission accomplishment), consisting of Objective 1.1, "Provide Science and Technology Results with Meaningful Impact on the Field," and Objective 1.2, "Provide Quality Leadership in Science and Technology that Advances Community Goals and DOE Mission Goals." For Objective 1.1, it

---

[75] NASA JPL, "Performance Evaluation and Measurement Plan/Award Term Plan, Performance Period October 1, 2018–September 30, 2019," signed September 28, 2018b, Not available to the general public. See also NASA JPL, Contract No. 80NM0018D0004P00002, Appendix 2, "The NASA Management Office Performance Appraisal Process: Performance Evaluation and Measurement Plan/Award Term Plan Preparation Guidance, July 26, 2018a, p.12, Not available to the general public. We obtained the contract from the NASA Management Office. A previous NASA JPL contract drew substantial criticism, but the current NASA JPL contract has a different structure. See, e.g., GAO, 2007; NASA, Office of the Inspector General, *NASA Should Reconsider the Award Evaluation Process and Contract Type for the Operation of the Jet Propulsion Laboratory*, Report No. IG-09-022-Redacted, September 25, 2009.

[76] The goals for all the directorates and offices that use the contract map directly to the CPARS language for grading areas, but not all the directorates and offices evaluate all the goals.

[77] Carol H. Weiss, *Evaluation Research: Methods of Assessing Program Effectiveness*, Englewood Cliffs, N.J.: Prentice-Hall, 1973.

[78] Weiss, 1973.

[79] See e.g., DOE and Ames Laboratory, 2018, and other DOE laboratory PEMPs.

also suggests considering, more specifically, the laboratory's performance with respect to proposed research plans, community impact and peer review, and impact on mission needs.[80]

In some instances, the PEMP for a DOE laboratory also includes site-specific "notable outcomes," tied to particular objectives. For example, Ames Laboratory's PEMP includes one notable outcome for Objective 1.1:

> Efficiently stand up the "Center for the Advancement of Topological Semimetals" Energy Frontier Research Center and deliver impactful science, as measured by the FY [fiscal year] 2019 management review and annual report, research publications and highlights, and participation in periodic conference calls and [a meeting].[81]

As a matter of policy, failure to obtain a notable outcome results automatically in a less-than-satisfactory grade for the related objective.[82]

By comparison, the NASA JPL PEMP works with goals that map directly to the FAR language but that also drill down to agency-specific objectives.[83] For example, under the first goal (on technical quality), the PEMP calls on JPL to provide "sound project management, system engineering, software engineering, mission assurance and logistics support in accordance with guidance provided by NASA" for the Science Mission Directorate.[84] For that directorate, the PEMP also includes three notable outcomes under "technical quality" (e.g., a successful spacecraft landing), but it does not appear to tie the outcomes to an objective.

The literature suggests the importance of connecting factors, as we define them, to concrete measures.[85] Therefore, if a grading factor cannot serve as measure—e.g., because it is insufficiently specific or is not rooted in verifiable observation—it should either be used to derive or be linked to a measure or measures in some way.

For example, Ames Laboratory's PEMP (among others) provides further guidance on assessing "meaningful impact," per Objective 1.1, and suggests that the

> evaluator(s) may consider the following as measured through progress reports, peer reviews, Field Work Proposals (FWPs), Program Office reviews/oversight, etc.:
>
> - Impact of publications on the field, as measured primarily by peer review;
> - Impact of S&T results on the field, as measured primarily by peer review;
> - Impact of S&T results outside the field indicating broader interest;

---

[80] DOE and Ames Laboratory, 2018.

[81] DOE and Ames Laboratory, 2018, p. 13.

[82] DOE and Ames Laboratory, 2018, p. 2.

[83] NASA JPL, 2018b.

[84] NASA JPL, 2018b.

[85] See, e.g., GAO, 2013, or Greenfield, Williams, and Eiseman, 2006.

- Impact of S&T results on DOE or other customer mission(s);
- Successful stewardship of mission-relevant research areas; Delivery on proposed S&T plans; Significant awards (Nobel Prizes, R&D 100, Federal Laboratory Consortium, etc.);
- Invited talks, citations, making high-quality data available to the scientific community;
- Development of tools and techniques that become standards or widely-used in the scientific community.[86]

The General Services Administration notes that universities' measures of academic performance and productivity are "frequently cited as a best practice model in discussions of knowledge worker productivity," partly because they focus on outcomes rather than solely on outputs, they tend to use systems that are "contextually valid" (meaning outcomes stem from organizational goals), and systems often capture measures from a variety of sources.[87]

A GAO report lists key attributes of successful performance measures that address matters of purpose, scope, and grading (Table 3.2).[88] Although the attributes are framed in terms of performance measurement, most of the attributes, including those pertaining to linkages, clarity, objectivity, reliability, and cost, bear on other dimensions of assessment.

---

[86] DOE and Ames Laboratory, 2018, p. 10.

[87] General Services Administration, *Knowledge Worker Productivity: Challenges, Issues, Solutions*, Washington, D.C., June 2011.

[88] GAO, 2013, pp. 22–23.

Table 3.2. Attributes of Successful Performance Measures

Attributes	Definitions	Potentially Adverse Consequences of Not Meeting Attribute
Linkage	Measure is aligned with division- and agency-wide goals and mission and clearly communicated throughout the organization.	Behaviors and incentives created by measures may not support achieving division- or agency-wide goals or missions.
Clarity	Measure is clearly stated, and the name and definition are consistent with the methodology used to create it.	Data may confuse or mislead users.
Measurable target	Measure has a numerical goal.	Managers may not be able to determine whether performance is meeting expectations.
Objectivity	Measure is reasonably free from significant bias or manipulation.	Performance reviews may be systematically overstated or understated.
Reliability	Measure produces the same result under similar conditions.	Reported performance data may be inconsistent and add uncertainty.
Core program activities	Measures cover the activities that an entity is expected to perform to support the intent of the program.	Information available to managers and stakeholders in core program areas may be insufficient.
Limited overlap	Measure provides new information beyond that provided by other measures.	Managers may have to sort through redundant, costly information that does not add value.
Balance	Taken together, measures ensure that an organization's various priorities are covered.	Measures may overemphasize some goals and skew incentives.
Governmentwide priorities	Each measure should cover a priority, such as quality, timeliness, or cost of service.	A program's overall success is at risk if all priorities are not addressed.

SOURCE: GAO, 2013, pp. 22–23.

The GAO report emphasizes quantification, but others take a broader stance on "empirics," or verifiable observation.[89] For example, some authors find that qualitative approaches can be used to understand how and why programs perform or underperform and that qualitative data can provide insight on their own or along with quantitative data.[90] Regardless of the form, the measures should focus on issues that matter and are, at least partly, within the control of those

---

[89] GAO, 2013. See also Landree, Miyake, and Greenfield, 2015; Eric Landree and Richard Silberglitt, *Application of Logic Models to Facilitate DoD Laboratory Technology Transfer*, Santa Monica, Calif.: RAND Corporation, RR-2122-OSD, 2018; Pun and White, 2005; Patricia J. Rogers and Delwyn Goodrick, "Qualitative Data Analysis," in Wholey, Hatry, and Newcomer, 2010; and W.K. Kellogg Foundation, *The Step-by-Step Guide to Evaluation: How to Become Savvy Evaluation Consumers*, Battle Creek, Mich., 2017.

[90] Rogers and Goodrick, 2010.

who are being measured.[91] Those who are being judged tend to focus on what they are being judged for, and they can only be judged fairly on what they can control.

Research also warns against measures that focus on a single, absolute threshold score (e.g., "95 percent of X"), noting that such thresholds can be appealing but prove to be problematic.[92] For example, low achievers with no prospect of reaching a threshold might give up, and high achievers who have already reached the threshold, or "topped out," might not try any harder. More generally, even good performance measures can top out in dynamic environments in which improvements in performance are both sought and obtained.

Although the DOE PEMPs provide examples of measures,[93] GAO has observed that DOE has not uniformly met the mark in this arena and points to some of the challenges of developing a well-honed, effective assessment process.[94] For example, in assessing the laboratories' "Work for Others" (WFO) program, GAO found that

> performance measures do not directly link with the WFO program goals or objectives such as providing access to DOE laboratories to accomplish goals that may be otherwise unattainable by federal agencies and nonfederal entities. Without such linkage, DOE and decision makers may not have the needed information to track the program's progress in meeting its objectives. Additionally, some WFO qualitative measures such as customer satisfaction may lack clarity and a measurable target, making it difficult to compare performance across laboratories. [They] also may not meet the key attribute of objectivity due to the potential for bias or other manipulation, depending on how the information is gathered and assessed. Other efforts to measure the performance of the program—specifically, the number of WFO agreements in place and WFO agreement processing time—both provide some helpful information but do not include all key attributes of successful performance measures. For example, tracking the number of agreements is clear and measurable and provides some information about the number of WFO projects at a laboratory. However, without linkage to the program's objectives, measuring the number of agreements in place does not capture the program's effectiveness in meeting the program's objectives laid out in the WFO order, such as maintaining core competencies and enhancing the science and technology base at the laboratories.[95]

The GAO report points to shortfalls in both qualitative and quantitative measures, suggesting that quantification by itself does not confer utility. Measurement for measurement's sake might incur costs but yield no or insufficient benefits.

---

[91] Stecher et al., 2010.

[92] Stecher et al., 2010.

[93] See, e.g., DOE and Ames Laboratory, 2018.

[94] GAO, 2013.

[95] GAO, 2013, p. 23.

In another report, GAO reminds readers that too much of a good thing (i.e., too many factors or subfactors) can be a bad thing.[96] Referring to award-fee determination, GAO makes a larger point about dilution, distraction, and administrative burden:

> The NASA award-fee guide cautions that spreading the potential award fee over a large number of performance evaluation factors dilutes emphasis on any particular performance evaluation criterion, increases the prospect of any one item being too small and thus overlooked, and increases the administrative burden. . . . Although the JPL performance evaluation plan characterizes award-fee subfactors as representing major areas of emphasis during the performance period, the award-fee subfactors . . . were numerous—96 subfactors were used to evaluate the contractor's performance in fiscal year 2004.[97]

That GAO report notes that NASA expected to get down to 45 "subfactors" (which we refer to as factors) by 2007.

Speaking to the practical, several RAND reports provide a logic model template that links operations to strategy and can be used to derive performance measures from an organization's strategy (including goals and objectives) and, as we discuss later, establish evidentiary needs to measure performance (Figure 3.1).[98] In that work, "objectives" tend to be more process-focused and "managerial" than goals, but the basic premise still holds.

---

[96] GAO, 2007.

[97] GAO, 2007, pp. 12–13.

[98] See, e.g., Greenfield, Williams, and Eiseman, 2006.

Figure 3.1. Logic Model Template

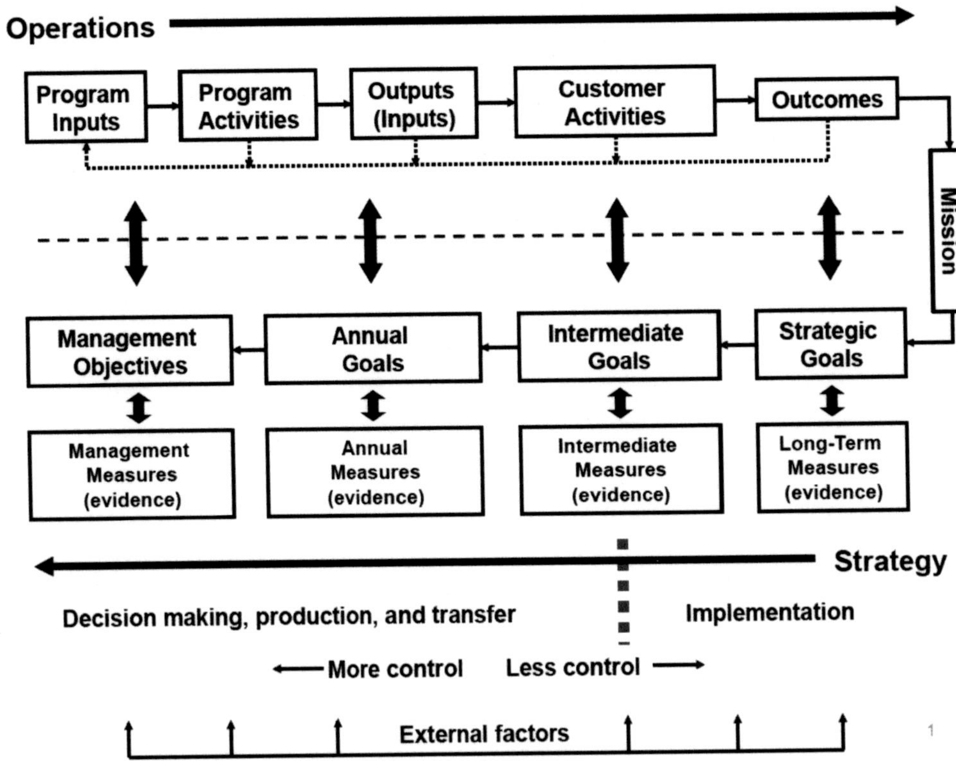

SOURCE: Greenfield, Shelton, and Balkovich, 2016, p. 4, adapting Greenfield, Williams, and Eiseman, 2006, p. 4.

As shown in Figure 3.1, inputs lead to activities, outputs, and, eventually, outcomes; objectives or goals map to each step along the path, and, for each objective and goal, performance measures gauge progress en route, with validation from evidence.[99]

To chart this path, this literature draws a distinction between "outputs" and "outcomes."[100] From a RAND report, "Outcomes . . . are the changes that occur and the benefits that result from the program activities and outputs. They involve changes in knowledge, attitudes, and behaviors . . . . [E]nd outcomes are the desired results of the program"; by comparison, "Outputs are the products (goods or services) that activities generate."[101]

---

[99] From Greenfield, Williams, and Eiseman, 2006, p. 5,

> A measure in and of itself does not demonstrate progress or results; rather, it provides a means of gauging progress or results. It is only by quantifying or qualifying each measure with "evidence" that a program can demonstrate its progress or results. Evidence, in effect, provides validation.

[100] For example, Greenfield, Williams, and Eiseman, 2006; Victoria A. Greenfield, Shoshana R. Shelton, and Edward Balkovich, *The Role of Logic Modeling in a Collaborative and Iterative Research Process: Lessons from Research and Analysis Conducted with the Federal Voting Assistance Program*, Santa Monica, Calif.: RAND Corporation, RR-882/1-OSD, 2016; Landree, Miyake, and Greenfield, 2015; and Williams et al., 2009.

[101] Greenfield, Shelton, and Balkovich, 2016, p. 5. See also Landree, Miyake, and Greenfield, 2015, p. 12, which discusses outcomes in the context of a federal nanotechnology research center: "End outcomes typically are societal,

To illustrate the basic approach, another RAND report constructs a logic model and derives performance measures for a sexual violence prevention program.[102] In that case, one goal of the program was to increase knowledge of violence prevention, and a measure for that goal considered participation in and test results from related training programs.

In reference to a more technologically complex environment, a study on technology transfer from DoD laboratories suggests "notional measures" for each element of a logic model but does not specify goals or objectives.[103] In consideration of the efficacy of technology transfer from those laboratories, the authors ask about the prevalence and quality of transfer mechanisms—consisting of prototype demonstrations, patent licensing, and publications—and follow up with questions about intake and use. Ultimately they are looking for evidence on new products or capabilities, new procedures or changes in practice, and subsequent efforts to generate systems, components, devices, and hardware or software that could make their way to final application. Similarly, a RAND pilot study on the impact of nanotechnology research also probes the efficacy of transfer mechanisms, intake, and use, with related evidence for each.[104]

Others offer a test for performance measures that touches on some of the same issues as GAO (Table 3.3).[105]

---

economic, or environmental benefits . . . [and] are closely connected to a program's strategic goals or stated mission."

[102] Greenfield, Williams, and Eiseman, 2006.

[103] Landree and Silberglitt, 2018.

[104] Landree, Miyake, and Greenfield, 2015.

[105] Neely, Adams, and Kennerley, 2002, pp. 38–45; GAO, 2013, pp. 22–23.

Table 3.3. Tests for Performance Measures

Test	Description
Truth	• Are we really measuring what we set out to measure?[a]
Focus	• Are we only measuring what we set out to measure?
Relevance	• Are we measuring the right thing?
Consistency	• Will different people apply the measure (e.g., collect data) in the same way?[b]
Access	• Are the data that inform a measure easy to locate, capture, and understand?
Clarity	• Can different people interpret the results in different ways?[c]
So-what?	• Does the measure provide the organization with actionable insights?[d]
Timeliness	• Can the data be analyzed and accessed quickly enough for timely action?
Cost	• Is the measure worth the cost of measurement?
Gaming	• Is the measure likely to encourage any undesirable or inappropriate behavior that runs contrary to the intent of the assessment or ultimate goals of the organization?[e]

SOURCE: Neely, Adams, and Kennerley, 2002, Figure 3.4, p. 45, with modest formatting and content changes, based on our interpretation of Neely, Adams, and Kennerley's supporting discussion on pp. 38–44. However, we did not modify the descriptions of the truth, focus, and cost tests. These descriptions are direct quotations, except for formatting changes.
[a] The truth, focus, and relevance tests cover different aspects of validity. For more on validity, see also Harry P. Hatry and Kathryn E. Newcomer, "Pitfalls in Evaluations," in Wholey, Hatry, and Newcomer, 2010, p. 558, and the discussion of process evaluation later in this chapter.
[b] This test—which we have interpreted more broadly than Neely, Adams, and Kennerley (2002, pp. 40 and 45), who focus on data collection—refers to internal reliability, and it allows replicability.
[c] Ideally, the results should be unambiguous and indisputable.
[d] An organization should ask and be able to answer, "Who acts on the data?" and "What do they do?," because "[m]easures that are not acted upon are simply a waste of time and effort" (Neely, Adams, and Kennerley, 2002, p. 41).
[e] Neely, Adams, and Kennerley (2002, p. 42) offer this example: "[I]f the level of output is introduced as a process measure, will quality be compromised by people taking short cuts?"

Lastly, we cite research that reminds organizations that seek to implement assessments that performance measures play a part in assessment, but are not themselves assessments: "[P]erformance measures do not, in their own right, constitute performance evaluations; rather, they are—or provide—essential inputs to performance evaluations."[106]

Grading Standards

To elicit an accurate and reliable assessment, surveys and other instruments should clearly define the meaning of a good or bad grade or evaluation score.[107] On a cautionary note,

> [Different raters] can have markedly different evaluation standards. Comparison ratings across work groups in an organization then become invalid. For example,

---

[106] Greenfield, Williams, and Eiseman, 2006, p. 5.

[107] Schiemann, 2009.

a rating of 6 from an "easy" [rater] may actually be lower in value than a rating of 4 from a more stringent [rater].[108]

In regard to this limitation of rating scales, others suggest that the "more precise the definition of factors and degrees, the more accurately the rater can evaluate . . . . It is important that each rater interpret factors and degrees the same way."[109] They call for performance appraisal training, but they also point out that evaluation forms need to describe what performance levels, such as "above expectations" or "below expectations," actually mean. Consistent with this point, guidance for the CPARS specifies that assessing officials should review the "proposed ratings and narratives to ensure ratings are consistent with the definitions in FAR 42.1503(h)(4) and narratives are detailed, comprehensive, complete, accurate, and supported by objective evidence wherever possible."[110] The FAR specifies a five-tier scale that ranges from "exceptional" to "unsatisfactory" (in which "satisfactory" represents the midpoint), with corresponding letter grades "A" through "E" and the potential for "pluses" and "minuses."

Some agencies that offer performance-based incentives include additional guidance on grading, apparently to discourage grade inflation.

The NASA JPL PEMP assigns letter grades "A" through "F" without pluses or minuses and offers the following instruction for grading on operational performance:

> Operational performance at the Laboratory meets NASA's expectations (defined as the grade of C) for each Objective if the Contractor is performing at a level that fully supports the Laboratory's current and future science and technology mission(s). Performance that has, or has the potential to, 1) adversely impact the delivery of the current and/or future NASA/Laboratory mission(s), 2) adversely impact NASA and or the Laboratory's reputation, or 3) does not provide the competent people, necessary facilities and robust systems necessary to ensure sustainable performance, shall be graded below expectations . . . . NASA sets our expectations high, and expects performance at that level to optimize the efficient and effective operation of the Laboratory. Performance that might merit grades above C would need to reflect a Contractor's significant contributions to the management and operations at the Laboratory, or recognition by external, independent entities as exemplary performance.[111]

Therefore, the NASA JPL PEMP establishes "C" as the operational norm and suggests that "A's" and "B's" are not to be handed out lightly.

Moving further up the grading scale and allowing for pluses and minuses, DOE establishes "B+" as the norm (that is, meeting expectations or requirements), and anything above a "B+"

---

[108] Luis R. Gómez-Mejía, David B. Balkin, and Robert L. Cardy, *Managing Human Resources*, Englewood Cliffs, N.J.: Prentice Hall, 1995, p. 261.

[109] R. Wayne Mondy, *Human Resource Management*, in collaboration with Judy Bandy Mondy, 12th ed., Boston, Mass.: Prentice Hall, 2011, p. 247.

[110] CPARS, 2018, p. 19.

[111] NASA JPL, 2018b; and NASA JPL, 2018a, p. 18. Note that the "Contractor" in this case is the California Institute of Technology, which operates JPL.

requires substantial justification and is all-but-disallowed for goals pertaining to M&O, similar to NASA's policy for operational performance.[112]

For grades on M&O goals,

> [p]erformance that might merit grades above B+ would need to reflect a Contractor's significant contributions to the management and operations at the system of Laboratories, or recognition by external, independent entities as exemplary performance.[113]

The laboratories' S&T goals are also pegged to "B+," although they are framed somewhat differently. Data from DOE's national laboratory assessments over the past decade show that the agency's grading tends toward "meeting expectations" or a rung higher, includes grades that are lower than "B+" (albeit infrequently), and results in very few straight "A's" or "A+'s" (Figures 3.2 and 3.3). Indeed, over that period, the agency did not award any "A+'s." However, it is unclear whether DOE grades along the entire scale or whether it mostly chooses between "B+'s" and "A−'s." For M&O, the process might yield its own version of grade inflation, in which "B+" is the highest likely grade—as the grade that yields full awards—and so "B+" is also the dominant grade.[114]

---

[112] The language on grading for M&O objectives in DOE's contracts with the national laboratories is nearly identical to the language in NASA's JPL contract and may predate that language; that is, NASA may have "borrowed" the language on grading and expectations from DOE.

[113] DOE and Ames Laboratory, 2018, p. 3.

[114] As noted previously, DOE has come under criticism for its oversight of the laboratories, including its M&O grading (GAO, 2019), which appears to suffer from a deficit of data.

Figure 3.2. Distribution of DOE Grades for National Laboratories' Science and Technology Goals

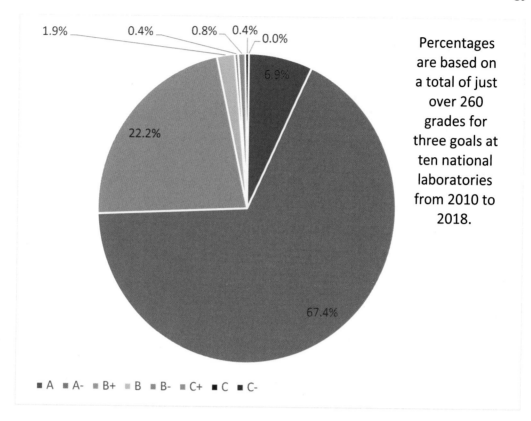

Percentages are based on a total of just over 260 grades for three goals at ten national laboratories from 2010 to 2018.

SOURCE: DOE, Office of Science, "Office of Science Lab Appraisal Process," webpage, undated.
NOTE: Although this breakout of grades for S&T goals shows more "A–'s" than "B+'s," a separate breakout for M&O goals shows the opposite (Figure 3.3), and pooled data show an almost even distribution of "B+'s" and "A–'s."

Figure 3.3. Distribution of DOE Grades for National Laboratories' Management and Operations Goals

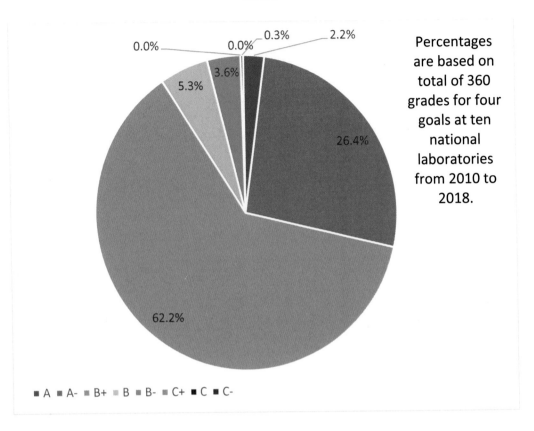

Percentages are based on total of 360 grades for four goals at ten national laboratories from 2010 to 2018.

SOURCE: DOE, undated.
NOTE: Although a separate breakout of grades for S&T goals shows more "A–'s" than "B+'s" (Figure 3.2), this breakout for M&O goals shows the opposite, and pooled data show an almost even distribution of "B+'s" and "A–'s."

Evidence

After officials decide on the purpose and scope of an assessment process and specify grading areas, factors, and related measures, they can focus on collecting evidence, measuring performance, and, eventually, putting evidence to use. To do so, they must identify evidence needs, sources, and means of elicitation. Here, too, the literature suggests that too much of a good thing can be a bad thing, partly for reasons of complexity and cost.[115] To use evidence for decisionmaking, an organization can take such steps as making comparisons among units, integrating data from different parts of the organization or from different programs, considering other ways of breaking out data, and using external benchmarking,[116] but first it must gather the right data from the right sources in the right way.

---

[115] GAO, 2007; Neely, Adams, and Kennerley, 2002.

[116] Theodore H. Poister, "Performance Measurement: Monitoring Program Outcomes," in Wholey, Hatry, and Newcomer, 2010.

Needs for Evidence

The performance appraisal literature commonly distinguishes among the evaluation of traits (worker characteristics, such as reliability, energy, and loyalty), behaviors or processes (actions taken at work), and outcomes (results or goals achieved at work), suggesting at least three different needs for data.[117] The programmatic literature tends to further distinguish between outputs (which precede outcomes) and outcomes themselves, and it also addresses matters of quality and efficiency.[118] If an organization is evaluating

- employee **traits**, then the data collection will tend to focus on identifying consistent and enduring characteristics of individuals.[119]
- employee- or group-level **behaviors**, then the data collection will tend to focus on what people do on the job: e.g., whether they help prepare for a briefing, whether they are accessible, and whether they are responsive to technical questions.[120]
- **outputs and outcomes**, then the data collection will tend to focus on workers' or a program's achievements and contributions to organizational goals. Outcomes, as noted earlier, involve the intended goals of a program, including changes to a process or environment that stem from outputs, whereas outputs are the products, services, or other work of a program, such as complete projects or risk assessments.[121]
- **service quality**, then the data collection may address "timeliness, turnaround time, **accuracy**, thoroughness, accessibility, convenience, courtesy, and safety."[122]
- **efficiency**, then the data collection will address the relationship between costs and outputs [or outcomes] or productivity and time frame.[123]

As GAO suggests, data collected to serve an organization's performance needs should be sufficiently robust to support objective, reliable analysis.[124]

In the context of FFRDC oversight, which does not concern employee-level appraisals, one might expect officials to focus more on the organizational equivalents of behaviors, outputs and outcomes, etc., than on traits, but not to the latter's exclusion, which could include an FFRDC's

---

[117] For example, Robert N. Lussier and John R. Hendon, *Human Resource Management: Functions, Applications, and Skill Development*, 3rd ed., Thousand Oaks, Calif.: SAGE Publications, 2019; Susanne G. Scott and Walter O. Einstein, "Strategic Performance Appraisal in Team-Based Organizations: One Size Does Not Fit All," *Academy of Management Executive*, Vol. 15, No. 2, 2001.

[118] For example, Greenfield, Williams, and Eiseman, 2006; Greenfield, Shelton, and Balkovich, 2016; and Poister, 2010.

[119] Lussier and Hendon, 2019; Scott and Einstein, 2001.

[120] Lussier and Hendon, 2019; Scott and Einstein, 2001.

[121] Landree, Miyake, and Greenfield, 2015; Poister, 2010.

[122] Poister, 2010, p. 103.

[123] Poister, 2010.

[124] GAO, 2013.

capability mix. Similarly, DoDI 5000.77 focuses on the assessment of an FFRDC's "technical quality, responsiveness, value, and timeliness."[125]

Research on program evaluation provides one method of deriving *evidentiary needs*: that is, the evidence that would be necessary to measure a program's progress at any point along the path from inputs to outcomes, which is depicted in Figure 3.1.[126] Two studies have applied this approach to DoD laboratories and nanotechnology research, respectively, looking for evidence of successful transfer in each case.[127] In the case of a DoD laboratory, evidence could range from patents, publications, and prototypes as early indicators to a fielded weapon system that incorporates elements of research from the laboratory.

Sources of Evidence

In the context of this report, sources of evidence include systems, processes, and people from which organizations draw empirical insight, either quantitative or qualitative, to inform grading factors or measures and substantiate an assessment.

Types of sources can include the following:

- **Transactions,** e.g., service requests, inventories, activity logs, incident reports, production records, **complaints** or accolades from customers, and other database inputs.[128] For example, an organization might be able to download tracking data on program or contract deliverables—including due dates and completion dates—from existing electronic sources.
- **Direct observation** of behavior, e.g., through behavioral monitoring or examination or other processes for monitoring and evaluating ongoing work.
- **Project or process "follow-up,"** meaning gathering data from stakeholders after a **project** or process is complete (for example, with after action reports, "hot wash" meetings, interviews, or other data collection).[129]
- **Customers, employees and other stakeholders,** who can provide feedback about ongoing projects or programs via surveys or other methods.[130]

One author recommends using existing data sources to which stakeholders have already committed (to the extent possible) and highlights both the need for and the implications of undertaking trend analysis.[131] In regard to trend analysis, an organization should take steps not

---

[125] DoDI 5000.77, 2018, p. 18.

[126] Greenfield, Williams, and Eiseman, 2006.

[127] Landree and Silberglitt, 2018; Landree, Miyake, and Greenfield, 2015.

[128] Poister, 2010.

[129] Poister, 2010.

[130] In this report, we do not provide guidance on specific methods of research, such as surveys or interviews, or data analysis, which is outside the scope of our activity.

[131] Poister, 2010. Stecher et al., 2010, also points to the relevance of existing sources.

only to select sources of data that can be used to inform factors or measures in the current period but also to maintain the integrity of data over time.

The collection of additional sources of comparative evidence, such as external case study or benchmark data, may also be warranted.[132]

Another consideration, when obtaining evidence internally, is the location of a source—or its role—within an organization. Some authors recommend that an organization ask "Who will use the data? Who will own the measure? Who will provide the data?"[133] These questions can enable an organization to determine the roles of those who assist with the performance assessment and who the organization should elicit data from. For example, some researchers suggest turning first to program managers for insight into contributions to impact, which requires a higher-level perspective, by asking them "to identify the most significant outcomes that occurred under the review period."[134] Outlining the roles of individuals and departments can also help reinforce accountability by assigning responsibility.[135]

As a general rule, evidence should be gathered to support the scope and purpose of the performance assessment process, and this process should support the larger PM system in terms of horizontal and vertical coordination.[136]

Lastly, we consider the possibility of *external* (or third-party) reviews, which are conducted by individuals or entities outside a program to provide an outside perspective on performance.[137] The reviews might be thought of as "sources of evidence" and the results as "evidence," but they must rely on sources of their own.

Expert review methods used by federal agencies include, for example,

> (1) **peer review**, which is commonly used to make judgments about the careers of individual staff members, the value of publications, the standing of institutions, and the allocation of funds to individuals, organizations, and fields of inquiry; (2) **relevance review**, which is used to judge whether an agency's programs are relevant to its mission; and (3) **benchmarking**, which is used to

---

[132] Poister, 2010.

[133] Neely, Adams, and Kennerley, 2002, p. 56.

[134] Williams et al., 2009, p. 47.

[135] Neely, Adams, and Kennerley, 2002.

[136] In this context, horizontal coordination means that decisionmaking across an organization serves to support organizational objectives, whereas vertical coordination refers to employees understanding how their roles contribute to organizational objectives and suggests that decisionmaking up and down the organization aligns with organizational strategy (Anthony A. Atkinson, John H. Waterhouse, and Robert B. Wells, "A Stakeholder Approach to Strategic Performance Measurement," *Sloan Management Review*, Vol. 38, No. 3, 1997).

[137] Trevor L. Brown, Matthew Potoski, and David M. Van Slyke, *Complex Contracting: Government Purchasing in the Wake of the US Coast Guard's Deepwater Program*, New York: Cambridge University Press, 2013, pp. 48–49, provides an overview of some advantages of third-party review, suggestions for implementation, and numerous references to literature and guidance in the defense contracting environment.

evaluate the standing of an organization, program, or facility relative to another (Ruegg and Feller, 2003).[138]

Although *peer review* is a term that connotes reviews of scientific journal articles, peer-review panels (or expert panels) are common in research and development assessment processes and are often used in federal agencies for evaluations of activities that are larger than individual research outputs, such as programs or projects.[139] In a 2009 report, RAND researchers describe two examples of peer-review-based systems: a "peer panel," which is composed of individuals who are subject-matter experts in the area under evaluation (hence, "peers") and a "mixed panel," which can consist of peers, similar to those found in the former, and other types of experts.[140]

Peer review panels can vary in terms of their formality, with some leeway as to how "external" is defined in relation to the program or a project, if not the organization.[141] For example, panels can include staff who work for the organization but are positioned outside the program under evaluation, as well as experts from outside the organization entirely. The former (i.e., organizational yet "external" peers) can provide feedback from colleagues who are knowledgeable in relevant subject areas and understand the institution but are not directly involved with the work being evaluated. An organization can also turn to partners (e.g., from industry) to provide feedback from their vantage point.

In general, the primary criteria for selecting panelists are their expertise, their lack of real or perceived conflicts of interest, and their willingness or ability to follow objective criteria developed prior to the review.[142] Transparency regarding the role of the panel and its participants may also be a consideration; for example, a government agency may opt for a high degree of transparency to inform and preserve its reputation with the public and policymakers.[143]

Additionally, an organization can bring in a contractor to provide a targeted or comprehensive outsider perspective.[144] By contracting with a consultancy (an FFRDC or a university, for example), an organization can obtain a rigorous assessment, potentially free from conflicts of interest. For examples, the National Academies conducted a three-year review of the National Institute for Occupational Safety and Health's (NIOSH's) research programs to enhance

---

[138] Williams et al., 2009, p. 4.

[139] Michael Scriven and Chris L. S. Coryn, "The Logic of Research Evaluation," *New Directions for Evaluation,* Vol. 2008, No. 18, Summer 2008; and Williams et al., 2009.

[140] Williams et al., 2009.

[141] Rosalie Ruegg and Gretchen Jordan, *Overview of Evaluation Methods for R&D Programs: A Directory of Evaluation Methods Relevant to Technology Development Programs,* Washington, D.C.: U.S. Department of Energy, Office of Energy Efficiency and Renewable Energy, March 2007.

[142] Ruegg and Jordan, 2007.

[143] Ruegg and Jordan, 2007.

[144] James B. Bell, "Contracting for Evaluation Products and Services," in Wholey, Hatry, and Newcomer, 2010.

the impact of programs that are focused on reducing workplace illnesses and injuries and making overall improvements to safety and health.[145] Using an independent panel of 14 multidisciplinary experts, which included occupational safety and health subject-matter experts, scientists, and industry representatives, the National Academies reviewed approximately 15 NIOSH programs over five years. In this case, constituting an external, mixed panel was practical, given the large scope and depth of the program evaluations that NIOSH needed.

As with any dimension of performance assessment, an organization must balance its assessment needs with the resources necessary to complete the assessment (as discussed earlier), and conducting assessments, including formal, comprehensive external reviews, can be costly. External reviews entail not just the immediate contracting cost but inevitably draw on internal resources, too. In addition to funding, resource considerations include the "time allowed for completion of the work, pertinent technical expertise, program and stakeholder cooperation, and access to important records and program materials."[146]

Elicitation of Evidence

Elicitation refers to how an organization gathers evidence from various sources. In some instances, elicitation may mean downloading data from a database to inform a factor or performance measure; in other cases, it may mean asking questions in different ways to produce data. To elicit evidence, an organization can turn to individuals within the organization, individuals outside the organization, or administrative databases, as noted earlier, but it might approach each source differently, depending on the context.

For example, NIOSH research programs reportedly took several approaches to gathering evidence on impact to support the National Academies' review.[147] In addition to accessing their records, the programs reached out by

> directly contacting intermediate customers (i.e., industry, trade associations, other federal agencies, state and local OSH [Occupational Safety and Health] agencies) to find out how specific outputs had been used; contacting partners to find out whether they were aware of and could cite changes in the workplace based on program work; following up with individuals or organizations that requested information from the research program; using search-engine tools (i.e., Google® search, LexisNexis®, Public Library of Science) to identify hits from

---

[145] For further details, see Centers for Disease Control and Prevention, "The National Academies Evaluation of NIOSH Programs," webpage, last reviewed March 26, 2018. See also National Research Council and Institute of Medicine Committee to Review the NIOSH Respiratory Disease Research Program, "Framework for the Review of Research Programs of the National Institute for Occupational Safety and Health," in *Respiratory Diseases Research at NIOSH: Reviews of Research Programs of the National Institute for Occupational Safety and Health*, August 10, 2007.

[146] Rossi, Freeman, and Lipsey, 1999, p. 76.

[147] Williams et al., 2009, p. 47.

searches for NIOSH report titles; and identifying patented technologies related to the specific research program.[148]

Research on performance assessment and program evaluation provides examples of questions that, although they were intended for other purposes, might be appropriate for FFRDC-related customer satisfaction surveys, interviews, or focus groups. These questions can—or should—track to grading areas or grading factors under consideration, or the questions can simply restate them. For example, one author, who addresses evaluation in the context of public-sector organizations, describes four types of question such organizations can use to assess effectiveness, efficiency, impact, and adherence to best practices (see Table 3.4).[149]

Table 3.4. Four Types of Performance Questions

Type	Question
Effectiveness	• "Did the [entity] achieve the results it set out to produce?"
Efficiency	• "Did the [entity] produce these results in a cost-effective way?"
Impact	• What did the [entity] itself accomplish? What is the difference between the actual outcomes and the outcomes that would have occurred if the agency had not acted?"
Adherence to best practices	• "How do the operations and practices of this organization or program compare with the ones that are known to be most effective and efficient?"

SOURCE: Behn, 2003.

Others offer a complementary approach to questioning *impact*, which they frame as a program's contribution to outcomes, that digs more deeply—and explicitly—into underlying causality. To evaluate those contributions, they suggest asking the following:

- "What outcomes have been achieved and why?"
- "What aspects of my program led to these outcomes?"
- "What factors in our program activities and resources influenced (and are influencing) results and in what ways?"
- "What external factors may have influenced results, and in what ways?"[150]

---

[148] Williams et al., 2009, p. 47.

[149] Behn, 2013.

[150] Greenfield, Williams, and Eiseman, 2006, p. 24; citing John A. McLaughlin, "Managing for Results, Reaching for Success: A New Paradigm for Planning and Evaluating PT3 Programs," PT3 Grantee Communications Center, U.S. Department of Education, 2001; and John A. McLaughlin, "An Introduction to Planning, Conducting, and Managing Your Program Evaluation," presentation to the U.S. Environmental Protection Agency, Pathogen Equivalency Committee, September 30, 2003.

A federal agency could translate these questions to assess an FFRDC's contributions. These questions probe not just the existence of outcomes but the reasons for them, including the specific contributions of the program and other influences to achieving them.[151]

If an organization elects to develop a performance assessment process that feeds into strategic planning and decisionmaking, the process will need to look ahead as well as behind. An organization can do so by examining how management decisions will affect performance in the future,[152] identifying possible threats to an organization's success,[153] or establishing long-term goals along with goal-focused action plans.[154] Some authors also advocate for incentivizing members of organizations to think about the distant future with visioning or forecasting methods.[155]

Whereas retrospective questions (e.g., regarding accomplishments in the prior year or months) can capture evidence of the level of past performance in relation to goals, expectations, or timelines, prospective questions can ask about variables that support forward-looking goals, such as innovation. Innovation-oriented questions tend to focus on organizational inputs that support both technical (research and development) and nontechnical (e.g., process) innovations or outputs (e.g., new products or findings or publications about new processes or products).[156]

Unintended Consequences

As with the adage that "you get what you measure," the evaluation literature warns of the potential for unintended consequences that can displace goals and yield perverse results.

Goal displacement, a technical term, can occur when measurement systems foster behaviors that do not support tangible goals, or actively oppose them. By one author's definition, such displacement occurs "when people will perform toward the measures but sacrifice the real program or organizational goals in the process."[157] For example, the author cites reports of

---

[151] In Greenfield, Williams, and Eiseman's (2006) model, "intended outcomes" represent manifestations of organizational goals (see Figure 3.1); therefore, achieving those outcomes would imply congruence with an organization's strategy. Weiss, 1973, further suggests looking at why in addition to how well a program functions.

[152] Andrew Likierman, "The Five Traps of Performance Measurement," *Harvard Business Review*, October 2009.

[153] Robert M. Grant, *Contemporary Strategy Analysis*, 8th ed., West Sussex, United Kingdom: Wiley, 2013.

[154] Pietro Micheli and Jean-Francois Manzoni, "Strategic Performance Measurement: Benefits, Limitations and Paradoxes," *Long Range Planning*, Vol. 43, No. 4, August 2010.

[155] Abiodun Adegbile, David Sarpong, and Dirk Meissner, "Strategic Foresight for Innovation Management: A Review and Research Agenda," *International Journal of Innovation and Technology Management*, Vol. 14, No. 4, August 2017. Additional examples of forecasting methods can be found at RAND Corporation, "Forecasting Methodology," webpage, undated.

[156] Keith Smith, "Measuring Innovation," in Jan Fagerberg, David C. Mowery, and Richard R. Nelson, eds., *The Oxford Handbook of Innovation*, Oxford, United Kingdom: Oxford University Press, USA, 2005.

[157] Poister, 2010, p. 108.

"collateral damage" from No Child Left Behind legislation, which heavily emphasized test scores as a performance metric for schools:

> These reported harmful effects include administrator and teacher cheating, student cheating, exclusion of low-performing students from testing, counseling low-performing students out of school systems, teaching to the test, narrowing of the curriculum, and declining teacher morale (Nichols and Berliner, 2007).[158]

To avoid goal displacement, an organization can try to, among other things, anticipate problems (e.g., negative behaviors, such as cheating, that could emerge as individuals or parts of an organization strive to meet goals), keep measures focused on outcomes and outputs, and keep measures relatively simple and practical.[159] The proposed "gaming" test in Table 3.3 (i.e., "Is the measure likely to encourage behaviors that run contrary to the intent of the assessment or goals of the organization?") could help address this concern, as might "pilot testing" (discussed later).[160]

Drawing from literature and guidance on risk assessment, we note that conventional thinking in that arena suggests assessing the potential for—or risk of—unintended consequences, establishing threshold levels of tolerance for those consequences, acting to mitigate or reduce risk to tolerable levels, and developing a remediation strategy for residual risks.[161]

Deliverables and Timelines

The PM system and program evaluation literatures both provide insight into the role of deliverables and timelines. At a high level, a PM system must address the timing of information flows in terms of the frequency and speed of reporting, in addition to the scope, aggregation, and integration of information.[162] It is a given that an FFRDC sponsor's formal performance assessment process must meet any mandated deadlines for deliverables, such as CPARS submissions, but the prior discussion of institutional prerequisites, alignment, and integration suggests the importance of tying assessments to larger institutional processes related to strategic planning and resources allocation decisions (Figure 2.2). Measures should relate to or derive

---

[158] Poister, 2010, p. 108, citing Sharon L. Nichols and David C. Berliner, *Collateral Damage: How High-Stakes Testing Corrupts America's Schools*, Cambridge, Mass.: Harvard Education Press, 2007; see also Stecher et al., 2010, for broader concerns about teaching to the test.

[159] Poister, 2010.

[160] Neely, Adams, and Kennerley, 2002, p. 45.

[161] See, e.g., Army Techniques Publication 5-19, *Risk Management*, Washington, D.C.: Headquarters, Department of the Army, April 2014; U.S. Department of Homeland Security Risk Steering Committee, "DHS Risk Lexicon: 2010 Edition," September 2010; and National Academies of Sciences, Engineering, and Medicine, *Reducing the Threat of Improvised Explosive Device Attacks by Restricting Access to Explosive Precursor Chemicals*, Washington, D.C.: National Academies Press, 2018.

[162] Aldónio Ferreira and David Otley, "The Design and Use of Performance Management Systems: An Extended Framework for Analysis," *Management Accounting Research*, Vol. 20, No. 4, December 2009.

from organizational goals, but they may also need to draw information from larger institutional processes and, at the proper time, inform those processes.[163]

By extrapolation, the literature on employee-level performance review can also provide insight into the timing of the assessment process, even if that literature is not directly related. Typical employee review cycles tend to occur annually, ideally with feedback provided in a relatively continuous or timely way throughout the year.[164]

That said, some organizations are tailoring their approach to provide more-timely feedback at more-frequent intervals. For example, Deloitte, a consultancy that does project-based work, reorganized employee-level reviews to occur at the end of projects (or quarterly for longer-term projects) to capture feedback on recent work.[165] A challenge with this approach is gathering and providing timely, project-driven feedback in a way that does not overburden the employees who are responsible for or subject to these reviews.

In the commercial sector, the desire for improved developmental feedback has led some businesses to move away from formal employee performance evaluations altogether and toward iterative, feedback-driven processes.[166] Some authors also note that *agile* goals (meaning goals and expectations that can be adapted to changing conditions) can be used to allow employees (or, in some cases, programs) to reorient as circumstances change during the year.[167]

The program evaluation literature suggests that the timing of evaluation procedures is also contextually dependent, which means there is no single, correct timeline.[168] In general, the timing of a program evaluation should align with the time frame of the given program: For example, a program evaluation might begin just prior to project commencement (e.g., during proposal and design phases) and end only after the program is complete.[169] This perspective on evaluation timing might not map onto an annual timeline, but it can give insight into how projects or programs could be assessed at different points in their life cycles.

From a project-oriented perspective, researchers suggest asking the following:

- When does the evaluation need to be completed? This question will help you identify a deadline for completing your evaluation.
- Does the program have an end date? This question will help you identify the timing for post-program data collection.

---

[163] Stecher et al., 2010.

[164] Adler et al., 2016.

[165] Marcus Buckingham and Ashley Goodall, "Reinventing Performance Management," *Harvard Business Review*, April 2015.

[166] Adler et al., 2016; Peter Cappelli and Anna Tavis, "The Performance Management Revolution," *Harvard Business Review*, October 2016; and DeNisi and Murphy, 2017.

[167] Adler et al., 2016.

[168] Acosta et al., 2013.

[169] Acosta et al., 2013.

- Is the program cyclical (e.g., runs for eight weeks twice a year)? This question will also help you identify the timing for data collection to coincide with program cycles.
  - If yes, when is the next time that the program will be offered?
  - If no, how many months has the program been operating?[170]

Although performance assessment is not the same as project evaluation, taking a project-oriented perspective could make sense for some elements of an agency's FFRDC performance assessment process. For example, in NASA's approach to managing its performance, which often concerns highly technical, project-based work,

- strategic goals are "timeless"
- strategic objectives that support strategic goals can remain in place for up to ten years
- other performance and priority goals that support strategic objectives can remain in place for two to four years
- annual performance indicators, of course, apply annually.[171]

This nested and temporally tiered system provides for near- and long-term oversight of project-based work, in compliance with GPRA, but could be used more generally with programs that have medium- and long-term intended outcomes on the horizon. NASA relies on monthly and quarterly surveillance activities within the annual review period, as well as "periodic, in-depth program or special purpose assessments" and "recurring or special assessment reports to internal and external organization."[172]

Stakeholder Interactions

Here, we consider two closely related stakeholder issues: specifically, buy-in and training. The literature suggests that an effective performance assessment process requires stakeholder acceptance and buy-in and that training matters,[173] both to impart essential knowledge and skills and to facilitate buy-in. Whether the discussion of buy-in should precede that of training, as it does in this section, is debatable. Although stakeholders cannot implement a process properly, absent knowledge and skills, they might not choose to implement it properly if they are not convinced of its merit. Stakeholders can include individuals as well as groups and other organizations "that can affect or be affected by an evaluation process or its findings."[174] For an FFRDC sponsor, likely stakeholders in a performance assessment include the leaders and staff who are part of the process, the sponsor's FFRDCs, and, possibly, industry partners.

---

[170] Acosta et al., 2013, p. 55.

[171] NASA, *FY 2019 Volume of Integrated Performance*, Washington, D.C., 2018, p. 6.

[172] NASA, 2018, p. 9.

[173] Atkinson, Waterhouse, and Wells, 1997; Stecher et al., 2010.

[174] John M. Bryson and Michael Q. Patton, "Analyzing and Engaging Stakeholders," in Wholey, Hatry, and Newcomer, 2010, p. 31.

Buy-In

Select lessons from the change management literature on gaining support for change can also apply to performance assessment; for example, one author on change management suggests that support from a credible "coalition" of leaders is critical.[175] From a PM perspective, leadership support for assessment processes could improve the likelihood of assessments being taken seriously and providing organizational value-added. Ideally, both senior leaders and lower-level leaders will actively support the vision for performance assessment.[176]

Good communication, which is another core tenet of change management, may also be critical to assessment.[177] Extrapolating from work on organizational change, one might argue that organizations must communicate—and stakeholders should understand and support—(1) the vision for the performance assessment process, which is akin to the vision for change, (2) the goals of the process, which are akin to the goals of change, and (3) the steps to achieving those goals.[178] However, other authors warn that communicating values and visions is not, on its own, enough to foster stakeholder understanding and support.[179] They stress the importance of focusing on facts, enlisting frontline supervisors to communicate with employees, and prioritizing face-to-face communication rather than large meetings or websites. For them, the message cannot come just from the top in broad terms but must be concrete and communicated directly to stakeholders.

Moreover, stakeholder participation and involvement might help overcome resistance or ambivalence and increase buy-in for performance assessment processes.[180] Some examples of participation in this context include involvement in goal development and in designing assessment measures or questions.[181] Taking a "negotiated accountability" approach can mean including stakeholders in determining what evidence to collect and identifying meaningful measures, goals, or targets, among other efforts.[182] Building up stakeholder interest in a performance assessment can also connect the concerns of stakeholders with the process itself.

---

[175] John P. Kotter, *Leading Change*, Boston, Mass.: Harvard Business Review Press, 2012.

[176] Pulakos, 2004.

[177] Kotter, 2012, speaks to communication in terms of change management.

[178] Keith A. Nitta, Sharon L. Wrobel, Joseph Y. Howard, and Ellen Jimmerson-Eddings, "Leading Change of a School District Reorganization," *Public Performance and Management Review*, Vol. 32, No. 3, 2009.

[179] George Cheney, Lars Thøger Christensen, Theodore E. Zorn, Jr., and Shiv Ganesh, *Organizational Communication in an Age of Globalization: Issues, Reflections, Practices*, 2nd ed., Long Grove, Ill.: Waveland Press, 2011.

[180] Morgen Johansen, Taehee Kim, and Ling Zhu, "Managing for Results Differently: Examining Managers' Purposeful Performance Information Use in Public, Nonprofit, and Private Organizations," *American Review of Public Administration*, Vol. 48, No. 2, February 2018; John P. Kotter and Leonard A. Schlesinger, "Choosing Strategies for Change," *Harvard Business Review*, Vol. 86, No. 7/8, July–August 2008; and Stecher et al., 2010.

[181] W.K. Kellogg Foundation, 2017; Pulakos, 2004.

[182] Poister, 2010, p. 122. See also Stecher et al., 2010.

Even if an organization does not deeply involve its workforce in process development, organizational leaders can still elicit employee feedback, learn about employee concerns, and, to the extent possible, use those concerns to inform the process.[183]

Additionally, both the change management and program evaluation literatures suggest working with internal process champions or change agents, such as project leaders, gatekeepers, and sponsors, to build support for change or, in this context, assessment.[184] These individuals can help establish or maintain the vision for a change (including a new assessment process), communicate to others, assist with participation in the change or process, facilitate the process of change, and support the assessment process in parts of the organization.[185]

If members of an organization do not support a change in the organization—or the assessment process—some may resist it because of "a desire not to lose something of value, a misunderstanding of the change and its implications, a belief that the change does not make sense for the organization, and a low tolerance for change."[186] Resistance to change has a negative connotation, yet some authors suggest that "resistance" oversimplifies "ambivalence" and that focusing on resistance as inherently negative overlooks the potentially positive intentions of some "resisters."[187] For example, an employee with frontline knowledge may recognize problems with a proposed change that more-senior leaders are unable to see.[188]

Finally, as indicated in a previous section in the context of prerequisites and in Chapter 4 in relation to "red flags," transparency matters not just in terms of why or how a process functions but also in terms of what it yields, as a matter of results and consequences.[189]

Training

Although training must occur eventually among all participants in the performance assessment process, leaders should be trained to understand the purpose and use of the process and the reasons for its relevance to the organization and should learn how to identify needs, call out and minimize errors, react to feedback or inputs, and, if needed, use automated

---

[183] Bryson and Patton, 2010.

[184] See Laurie K. Lewis, Amy M. Schmisseur, Keri K. Stephens, and Kathleen E. Weir, "Advice on Communicating During Organizational Change: The Content of Popular Press Books," *Journal of Business Communication*, Vol. 43, No. 2, 2006, on change management and Bryson and Patton, 2010, on program evaluation.

[185] Lewis et al., 2006.

[186] Kotter and Schlesinger, 2008, p. 132.

[187] Florian E. Klonek, Nale Lehmann-Willenbrock, and Simone Kauffeld, "Dynamics of Resistance to Change: A Sequential Analysis of Change Agents in Action," *Journal of Change Management*, Vol. 14, No. 3, 2014.

[188] Sandy Kristin Piderit, "Rethinking Resistance and Recognizing Ambivalence: A Multidimensional View of Attitudes Toward an Organizational Change," *Academy of Management Review*, Vol. 25, No. 4, 2000.

[189] See, e.g., Moynihan, 2008.

components.[190] The first "should" implies a need for knowledge of the process, and the second implies a need for knowledge of the process as well as the skills to implement it.[191]

Training, as noted earlier, can also provide a venue for encouraging buy-in to the assessment process. Employee trainings can be used to communicate the vision for the process, which can help motivate employees to participate in and use the results from the assessment. However, as noted previously, vision alone is unlikely to get everyone on board without supporting facts and, in this or any context, some assurance that the process really matters.[192]

Although the medium for delivering content may vary (for example, classroom learning that occurs at set intervals versus online learning, which can occur on demand), research on the core components of topical coverage suggests including the following:

- Philosophy, vision, and uses of the system.
- Description of the annual review timeline, process, and other logistics.
- Role and responsibilities of senior leaders, managers, and employees.
- How expectations and goals are set.
- How to provide accurate evaluations, minimizing rating errors and inflation.
- The importance of ongoing, constructive, specific feedback.
- How to seek feedback effectively from others . . . .
- How to give feedback in a manner that minimizes defensiveness and/or retaliation.
- How to identify and address gaps in performance and organizational development needs.
- How to use the automated system and related software.[193]

First, training should occur at the highest organizational levels so that leaders gain a better understanding of the system, the extent of their involvement, and needs for additional support.[194] In the initial phases of the system's rollout, additional resources, such as help-desk or hotline support, may improve efficiency, reduce frustration, and enable quick fixes.[195] Eventually, training should be provided for participants at all levels of the organization that enables them to serve their roles and meet their responsibilities with appropriate skills, but the organization

---

[190] Pulakos, 2004. Additionally, Allas et al., 2018, stresses the importance of involving experts and training at all organizational levels, stating that "new capabilities are typically needed at all levels of the organization to deliver and sustain change" (Tera Allas, Martin Checinski, Roland Dillon, Richard Dobbs, Andres Cadena, Eoin Daly, David Fine, Solveigh Hieronimus, Navjot Singh, and John Hatwell, *Delivering for Citizens: How to Triple the Success Rate of Government Transformations*, New York: McKinsey, June 2018, p. 56).

[191] Jessie Riposo, Guy Weichenberg, Chelsea Kaihoi Duran, Bernard Fox, William Shelton, and Andreas Thorsen, *Improving Air Force Enterprise Resource Planning-Enabled Business Transformation*, Santa Monica, Calif.: RAND Corporation, RR-250-AF, 2013, pp. 26 and 58, also distinguishes between knowledge and skills.

[192] See the discussion in Chapter 4 on red flags and consequences.

[193] Pulakos, 2004, p. 27.

[194] Riposo et al., 2013, p. 26.

[195] Riposo et al., 2013, p. 26.

should not neglect to reiterate the vision of the system, goals of the system, and strategies for accomplishing the goals.[196] Throughout, trainings should involve experts and provide opportunities to ask questions and provide feedback, surface new issues, and give employees organizational voice.[197] In addition, information conveyed during trainings should be well-documented.[198]

Process Automation

Assessment processes should be automated to the extent that resources and other constraints (such as information security) allow.[199] Basic automation means creating online interfaces for conducting performance assessments and displaying information and rating systems, among other processes, that are consistent across the organization.[200] More-advanced automation can

- capture work products and documentation from staff over time
- help manage the workflow of the assessment process
- support real-time training or feedback on the assessment process (e.g., to reduce bias in the process, such as rating inflation)
- produce automated outputs or reports[201]
- include repositories of suggestions for future development and program needs
- facilitate decisionmaking by providing outputs that feed into other decisionmaking processes.

Automation can also assist users in bringing together multiple data points to provide a multidimensional perspective for a grading area or factor.[202]

A potential hazard of automation is *ossification*, or the inflexibility that can arise if an organization does not adjust the performance assessment over time or allow individuals to tailor their assessments in a way that avoids generalized responses that do not shed light on actual

---

[196] John P. Kotter, "Leading Change: Why Transformation Efforts Fail," in Joan V. Gallos, ed., *Organization Development,* San Francisco, Calif.: Jossey-Bass, 2006. For more on specific approaches to skill development, see also Harvard Business Review, *HBR Guide to Performance Management*, Boston, Mass.: Harvard Business Review Press, 2017.

[197] Cynthia L. King, Douglas Brook, and Timothy D. Hartge, *Effective Communication Practices During Organizational Transformation: A Benchmarking Study of the U.S. Automobile Industry and U.S. Naval Aviation Enterprise*, Monterey, Calif.: Naval Postgraduate School, No. NPS-CDMR-GM-07-001, July 2007. See also Allas et al., 2018, p. 56, on technical expertise.

[198] Pulakos, 2004.

[199] Bernard Marr, *Strategic Performance Management: Leveraging and Measuring Your Intangible Value Drivers*, Burlington, Mass.: Butterworth Heinemann, 2006.

[200] Pulakos, 2004.

[201] These first four points are drawn from Pulakos, 2004.

[202] Marr, 2006.

behaviors or events.[203] A performance assessment should balance alignment with local adaptation to avoid being too rigid and therefore less informative.[204]

Process Checks

In this section, we discuss two types of process checks, one at the "front end" of the process (i.e., pilot testing) and one "along the way" or at the "back end" (i.e., process evaluation). However, it would be wrong to think of either as strictly fixed in time, insomuch as changes should be validated and processes should be reconsidered continually. A performance assessment process, once created, should not be treated as a static process; rather, an organization should evaluate the effectiveness of the process and make improvements over time.

Pilot Testing

Pilot testing is a way of checking how well a performance assessment process will meet organizational needs.[205] Pilot tests can be conducted at a smaller scale in a subset of offices, departments, or some other subsection of the organization prior to full-scale implementation.[206] Moreover, as some authors suggest, participants should be representative, at least in terms of skill level and role, because only assessing the top performers could bias results.[207] It is considered good practice to test-run the entire assessment process from beginning to end, with the caveat that test results are not to be filed as actual performance data.[208] This way, the pilot test can shed light on problems that can be corrected prior to implementing a full, formal performance assessment.[209]

For example, pilot efforts can be used to look out for issues related to

- training processes, in terms of how well those conducting the performance assessment can follow through effectively[210]
- leadership support and understanding for the performance assessment process[211]
- user reactions to the performance assessment process[212]

---

[203] Micheli and Manzoni, 2010.

[204] Micheli and Manzoni, 2010.

[205] Aguinis, 2009; Aguinis, 2013; Pulakos, 2004.

[206] Aguinis, 2013; Pulakos, 2004.

[207] Hatry and Newcomer, 2010.

[208] Aguinis, 2013.

[209] Stecher et al., 2010.

[210] Pulakos, 2004.

[211] Pulakos, 2004.

[212] Aguinis, 2013; Pulakos, 2004.

- costs (time, money, etc.) in relation to benefits (improved decisionmaking) that stem from the performance assessment process[213]
- Problem areas (such as poorly defined or targeted measures) or undesirable outcomes (such as teaching to the test).[214]

Some authors suggest the inevitability of trial and error when developing assessment processes, given their complexity, and note that organizations should anticipate a need for refinement but that pilot testing can help head off problems early on.[215] In addition, they raise the possibility of implementing a process in stages: for example, by focusing on capacity-building first, then introducing performance measures and, eventually, incentives.[216]

Process Evaluation

An organization should evaluate the effectiveness of its assessment process while the assessment is in progress and periodically thereafter to gauge the extent to which the assessment measures performance in a way that is credible, valid, and reliable; incentivizes positive behaviors and disincentivizes negative behaviors; and provides information that feeds back into organizational goals and strategy and informs decisionmaking.[217]

Research on program evaluation suggests that a performance assessment process should adhere to the following tenets of methodological integrity:

- **Credibility**. Are the results of the process "believable and legitimate"?
- **External validity**. Are the results of the process generalizable to groups or settings beyond those being assessed?
- **Internal validity**. Does the process accurately capture cause-and-effect relationships? For example, can it describe how a change in a program activity or the introduction of a new program activity resulted in certain outcomes?
- **Measurement validity**. Is the organization measuring what it intends to measure?
- **Reliability**. If measurement procedures are repeated under the same or similar conditions, will the results be the same or similar?
- **Evidence conclusion validity**. Do the results, whether quantitative or qualitative, reflect good practices for conducting analyses and reporting on findings?[218]

---

[213] Aguinis, 2013; Stecher et al., 2010.

[214] Stecher et al., 2010; Aguinis, 2013; and Karin Martinson and Carolyn O'Brien, "Conducting Case Studies," in Wholey, Hatry, and Newcomer, 2010.

[215] Stecher et al., 2010.

[216] Stecher et al., 2010, addresses staging in the context of a larger performance-based accountability system, but the observation could apply equally in this narrower, yet still complex, context.

[217] Aguinis, 2009; Hatry and Newcomer, 2010; Smither and London, 2009; Stecher et al., 2010.

[218] We have drawn the content of these bullets from Hatry and Newcomer, 2010, p. 558, Box 23.1, "The Touchstones of Methodological Integrity," but we have adapted the content slightly for our purposes. For example, Hatry and Newcomer's final touchstone is "statistical conclusion validity," which we have reframed as "evidence conclusion validity" to accommodate qualitative analysis and results.

These tenets apply to performance assessments, as well as program evaluations, because of their similar reliance on data-gathering, empirical analysis of measures, and reporting, as compared to individuals' subjective views.

The program evaluation literature also provides lessons for checking on performance assessments while they are in progress to identify errors or challenges in real time.[219] Lessons for performance assessment include the following:

- An organization might gather too much data without enough time for analysis, particularly if there are delays in data collection or analysis proceeds slowly.
- Assessment measures may not work as well as expected, especially if programs change over time; thus, assessors should adjust or be prepared to adjust.
- Sources of evidence can shift, such that the "right source" is no longer "right."[220]
- An assessment might fail to account for—or misunderstand—the implications of a program's status or maturity; for example, a new program is more likely to be unstable than a long-lived program; therefore, assessing a program at inception would provide a different picture of performance than assessing it later would.
- Involving inappropriately interested—or self-interested—stakeholders in data collection can yield flawed data and might not shed light on program outcomes.
- Data collection procedures can artificially change behaviors; for example, selecting the top-performing employees in an organization to pilot a new program may mean that the results of the pilot are not generalizable across the organization.
- If participation or completion rates drop off in data collection or participants do not constitute a representative sample, the results could be incomplete or biased.[221]

The literature also recommends reflecting on performance assessments after they are complete to learn whether and how much the assessment process is serving its intended purposes.[222] A strategically oriented process should provide information that offers insight into organizational priorities, goals, and concerns and that informs decisionmaking. Thus, a retrospective look at the performance assessment process should be conducted to gauge the extent to which the PM system, including the assessments, supports this cycle.

Participants' feedback can be used to evaluate and improve the performance assessment process.[223] Responses to survey questions about the experiences of leaders, managers, and employees with the system can lead to potential modifications of the assessment process that will increase the usability.[224] This type of survey can include questions on whether employees find

---

[219] For example, Hatry and Newcomer, 2010.

[220] Similarly, performance measures can "top out" (Stecher et al., 2010, p. 182).

[221] These bullets synthesize various discussion points in Hatry and Newcomer, 2010, pp. 559–580.

[222] For example, Aguinis, 2009; Aguinis, 2013; and Silverman and Muller, 2009.

[223] Aguinis, 2009.

[224] Pulakos, 2004.

the process relevant and useful and whether it fits into the culture of the organization.[225] The survey can be retrospective and prospective, in the sense that it gathers both information about past experiences with the assessment process and recommendations for changes in the evaluation process.[226] An organization should use these surveys sparingly and be transparent about the results.[227] If employees are surveyed too often and results are not shared or visibly acted on, employees might experience survey fatigue (respondents get tired of taking surveys or drop out of surveys), leading to low response rates in future surveys.[228]

In addition, the quality of a performance assessment can be gauged by examining such factors as the number of units (i.e., individuals or programs) that have been evaluated, the distribution of performance ratings across units, the quality of information gathered, the quality of discussions about the assessment, the cost and benefits of the assessment, and comparisons of unit- and organization-level performance across areas or factors.[229] Data pertaining to the completion and attendance of trainings on the purpose and use of the assessment process can also be recorded, along with data on the completion of assessment activities.[230] This type of information can be cataloged and used for ex post analysis of the process.[231] Some authors also suggest using third-party reviews to evaluate the assessment process, not just to assess the performance of an organization or its contract support.[232]

Summary of Operational Criteria

We conclude this chapter with a summary of criteria for establishing and implementing an effective performance assessment process and related actions. With these *operational criteria*, we single out the characteristics—in terms of concept, design, and implementation—of an effective performance assessment process, taking the institutional prerequisites as given. By dealing with conceptualization (or "vision") at the outset, an organization can ask and answer two fundamental questions: specifically, what does it want from the assessment, and can the process provide it? Conceptualization necessarily spills over into design and implementation because it sets the stage for what topics (or "areas") to evaluate and how to evaluate them (e.g., with what "factors" and measures and by whom). Although the literature suggests that efficiency

---

[225] Pun and White, 2005; Schiemann, 2009.

[226] Charles A. O'Reilly and Michael L. Tushman, "Organizational Ambidexterity: Past, Present, and Future," *Academy of Management Perspectives*, Vol. 27, No. 4, November 2013.

[227] Pulakos, 2004.

[228] Neely, Adams, and Kennerley, 2002.

[229] Aguinis, 2009.

[230] Pulakos, 2004.

[231] Richard C. Larson and Leni Berliner, "On Evaluating Evaluations," *Policy Sciences*, Vol. 16, No. 2, 1983.

[232] Stecher et al., 2010.

should not be the sole criteria of performance assessment, it also recognizes that assessment is costly. For that reason, one might—or "should"—also consider efficacy, necessity, and sufficiency throughout.

Tables 3.5 through 3.8 draw from the best practices on operational criteria set out in this chapter; related findings on institutional prerequisites, including those on strategic alignment, process integration, and communication; and principles of efficacy and efficiency. Collectively, the tables cover conceptualization, design and implementation, stakeholder interaction, and process functionality and checks.

Table 3.5. Criteria, Actions, and Guiding Questions for *Conceptualizing* the Assessment Process

Process Phase or Characteristic	Criteria	Actions	Guiding Questions
Purpose	• Is clear and disseminated • Is shared by stakeholders • Fills needs administratively by satisfying regulatory or other formal requirements • Fills needs strategically by supporting organizational priorities, goals, etc. • Fills needs expeditiously	• Specify, disseminate, and socialize reasons—"why?"—for assessment (e.g., compliance, tracking, influencing behavior, planning and resource allocation)	• Is purpose clearly articulated, disseminated, and well-socialized? • Does purpose reflect priorities and satisfy requirements? • Can other tools meet needs better than performance assessment?

Scope	• Is clear and disseminated
	• Is shared by stakeholders
	• Is consistent with purpose and able to serve purpose
		• Specify, disseminate, and socialize terms of engagement—"who, what, where, and when?" including topical and functional coverage for "grading areas" (see Table 3.6)—of assessment	• Is scope clearly articulated, disseminated, and well-socialized?
			• Is scope "built to purpose"?
			  – Do areas of inquiry and investigation (e.g., as embodied in "grading areas", see Table 3.6) align with purpose?
			  – Can process support "prospective assessment" to feed into strategic planning and resource allocation processes?

52

Table 3.6. Criteria, Actions, and Guiding Questions for *Designing and Implementing* the Assessment Process

Process Phase or Characteristic	Criteria	Actions	Guiding Questions
Grading areas	• Are clear and disseminated • Are shared by stakeholders • Track to and support purpose and scope (see Table 3.5)	• Specify, disseminate, and socialize discrete grading areas that reflect purpose and embody areas of inquiry and investigation	• Are grading areas clearly articulated, disseminated, and well-socialized? • Do grading areas cover topics, issues, etc. that will serve purpose administratively, strategically, and expeditiously? • Do grading areas cover topics, issues, etc. that are fielded under scope?
Grading factors	• Are clear and disseminated • Are shared by stakeholders • Address organization's underlying priorities, goals, and concerns in each grading area • Constitute or provide basis for deriving "performance measures"	• Establish, disseminate, and socialize grading factors that track to priorities, goals, and concerns in each grading area and support performance measurement	• Are grading factors clearly articulated, disseminated, and well-socialized? • Do factors address organization's underlying priorities, goals, and concerns in each grading area? • Are factors used as, or can they be used to construct, indicators that are empirical, objective and unbiased, reliable, and valid? • Are factors and indicators nonrepetitive and balanced?
Grading standards	• Are clear and disseminated • Are shared by stakeholders • Are applied consistently • Are unbiased, without propensity toward low or high grading	• Establish, disseminate, and socialize definitions for "good" and "bad" grades and guidance on application, including evidentiary needs, that does not favor high or low grades	• Are grading standards clearly articulated, disseminated, and well-socialized? • Do stakeholders know what grades (e.g., "satisfactory") mean, and can they recognize corresponding performance? • Is process likely to favor high or low grading, e.g., with asymmetric burden of proof or follow-up?
Needs for evidence	• Represent necessary and sufficient information to evaluate each factor and/or performance measure empirically, objectively and without bias, reliably, and validly	• Identify necessary, sufficient, and appropriate evidence for purpose (e.g., compliance, tracking, influencing behavior, planning, and resource allocation) for each grading factor and/or performance measure	• What types of evidence (quantitative or qualitative) are necessary, sufficient, and appropriate for retrospective and prospective assessment? • How much evidence is enough, and what resources (e.g., financial or time) are needed to get it?

53

Process Phase or Characteristic	Criteria	Actions	Guiding Questions
Sources of evidence	• Provide information from which to draw necessary, sufficient, empirical, objective and unbiased, reliable, and valid evidence	• Identify extant and new sources of evidence, including individuals, groups, databases, and third parties	• Can individuals or groups provide evidence, and how might their roles differ according to their placement, including their level, in the organization? • Can existing data (e.g., in administrative databases) fill needs? • What part can third parties play? • How many sources are enough, and what resources (e.g., financial or time) are needed to access them?
Elicitation of evidence	• Yields necessary, sufficient, empirical, objective and unbiased, reliable, and valid evidence for evaluating each factor and/or performance measure	• Develop surveys, questionnaires, or other tools to elicit evidence from sources, including individuals, groups, and databases that track grading areas and factors • Develop surveys, questionnaires, or other tools to address future organizational needs and evaluate trends in related data that track grading areas and factors	• Are questions sufficiently specific and tied to evidentiary needs? • Do questions address both retrospective (past year's performance) and prospective areas (e.g., near-term or long-term considerations)? • Do participants understand questions and vocabulary (e.g., "outputs," "outcomes," and "impact") and the meaning of "evidence"?[a] • Are costs of elicitation reasonable in relation to anticipated gains?
Unintended consequences	• Are assessed for potential and mitigated or treated, consistent with threshold levels of tolerance	• Identify potential unintended consequences, establish tolerance, and mitigate or treat, as needed • Apply "gaming test" • Undertake pilot testing (see Table 3.8)	• What are likely unintended consequences? • What is your level of tolerance for unintended consequences? • How can unintended consequences be avoided, mitigated, or treated?
Deliverables and timelines	• Meet compliance needs and draw from and/or feed into other institutional processes	• Specify types and contents of deliverables, with illustrations and related due dates that are in synch with compliance and other institutional processes (e.g., strategic planning and resource allocation)	• Do deliverables satisfy regulatory and policy requirements? • Can deliverables feed into other institutional processes? • Will they provide necessary and sufficient content? • Will they arrive on time?

[a] This question derives from the earlier discussion of ambiguity and clarity of measures. Essentially, an organization should define its terminology clearly. Moreover, it might be helpful to use feedback to gauge whether and how well participants understand terminology.

Table 3.7. Criteria, Actions, and Guiding Questions for *Stakeholder Interactions* in the Assessment Process

Process Phase or Characteristic	Criteria	Actions	Guiding Questions

Buy-in	• Yields confidence in the assessment process, including belief in its legitimacy and expectations of positive value-added	• Cultivate stakeholder buy-in by
		  – Communicating "why?" and facts about assessment process
		    ▪ Signaling leadership support
		    ▪ Working with "change agents" and/or "process champions"
		    ▪ Engaging directly (e.g., face to face)
		  – Soliciting, obtaining, and responding to feedback on performance assessment process
		    ▪ Involving them in designing the assessment process
		    ▪ Seeking out and listening to "resisters"
		  – Sharing results of assessments and demonstrating potential for consequences
			• Who/what are stakeholders?
			• Which stakeholders matter at which points in process and why?
			• Do stakeholder know "why," "what," "how," etc.?
			• Do stakeholders have a role or voice in the process at outset and over time?
			  – How does the organization engage with stakeholders (e.g., modes of participation, channels, messages, frequency of communication)?
			  – How does the organization elicit and make use of feedback?
			• Is the process transparent and credible: e.g., can stakeholders observe results and consequences?

Training	• Imparts knowledge and skills to participate constructively in the performance assessment process and can yield buy-in	• Develop and plan approach to training
		  – Establish training priorities
		  – Tailor approach (e.g., by type or level of recipient) to train participants to understand why and how, fill their role, provide data or evidence, etc.
		• Solicit, obtain, and respond to participants' feedback about training and performance assessment
			• How is training conducted?
			• How should training be tailored for different types of participants across the organization?
			• How should training be allocated (e.g., who or which groups should be trained first, second, third)?
			• Does training cover appropriate material and topic areas?
			  – Do participants understand the need for and their roles in the assessment process?
			  – Do they know what to do, when to do it, and how?
			  – Do they have the necessary skills?
			• Does the organization solicit, obtain, and respond to feedback from participants about the training and assessment?

Table 3.8. Criteria, Actions, and Guiding Questions for *Process Functionality and Checks* in the Assessment Process

Process Phase or Characteristic	Criteria	Actions	Guiding Questions
Process automation	• Allows for timely and consistent data collection, analysis of results, and throughput to and connectivity with other institutional processes	• Develop automated procedures for delivering and collecting assessments, collating and analyzing evidence and results, and communicating with other institutional processes	• To what extent is the assessment process automated, or can it be automated? • If the assessment process is automated, – Does it improve workflow, facilitate analysis, etc.? – Does it obstruct dynamism or preclude tailoring? – Can the assessment process "talk" to other processes? • If the assessment process is not automated, what are the impediments?
Pilot testing	• Occurs as validation before launching a full-scale assessment and with significant process changes	• Conduct small-scale test runs to uncover shortcomings and avoid missteps that can drain resources, reduce efficacy, and impede stakeholder buy-in	• Is pilot testing on agenda for new or revamped process and, if so, – Who are "representative" participants? – What will they assess? • How will results be used: e.g., how will organization make use of data from pilot tests to improve procedures?
Process evaluation	• Provides the means to regularly assess, improve, and update the assessment process, including through stakeholder feedback	• Ensure performance assessment process adheres to tenets of methodological integrity • Monitor assessment process to improve it and adapt to changes in needs, with input from stakeholders • Solicit feedback from employees or gather other indicators to examine how well the assessment process functions	• Does the assessment process fulfill the tenets of methodological integrity, including validity and reliability? • Is process evaluation "built in"? • Is the organization watching for and taking steps to correct problems that arise during assessments? • Is the organization soliciting, obtaining, and responding to feedback about the performance assessment process? • How is the organization using feedback to improve the performance assessment process?

4. Potential Weaknesses of Performance Management Systems and Assessment Processes

As we addressed in the previous chapters, effective PM systems support organizational performance by linking goal-setting, performance measures, and reward systems in ways that support desired outcomes, such as impact or innovation, but not all systems succeed in whole or in part.[233] For example, according to some authors, attempts to measure performance tend to fail when they are designed poorly or when implementation is challenging.[234] The literature points to the following symptoms of poor performance system design that pertain to performance measurement and broader, systemic issues:

- Performance data are not used to inform decisionmaking or other actions.[235]
- Data might be collected and not used because of "information overload" or because the data or results lack relevance.[236]
- Tasks feel like rituals without substance.[237]
- Systems are too time-consuming or unhelpful.[238]
- There is a lack of transparency.[239]
- There is a lack of relevance to stakeholders.[240]
- There is a lack of consequences or accountability, meaning results provide negative feedback but individuals, groups, or business units are not held accountable.[241]
- Internal organizational politics contradict PM systems.[242] For example, results from an assessment might be contradicted by the internal politics of the organization's leaders.

Just as we were able to draw insight into best practices, institutional prerequisites, and operational criteria from the positive, we can draw insight from the negative. Here, the literature warns us against the possibilities of fruitless, irrelevant, and unused measurement and, by implication, points to the necessity of follow through.

---

[233] Moynihan, 2008.

[234] Pun and White, 2005.

[235] Andrew Neely and Mike Bourne, "Why Measurement Initiatives Fail," *Measuring Business Excellence*, Vol. 4, No. 4, December 2000; as cited in Pun and White, 2005.

[236] Moynihan, 2008.

[237] Moynihan, 2008.

[238] Moynihan, 2008.

[239] Moynihan, 2008.

[240] Moynihan, 2008.

[241] Moynihan, 2008.

[242] Moynihan, 2008.

In large part, the negatives reinforce the lessons of the positives, but they offer a few new insights. In particular, they point to the interrelated importance of stakeholders' buy-in, including perceptions of the efficacy of the assessment process, the value of time, and the role of consequences. If stakeholders view the assessment process as ineffectual and a waste of their time, they are unlikely to devote much attention to it; if the process is free of any consequences (good or bad), they might not see the potential for an effect.[243]

Thus, the presentation of symptoms of failure (in addition to signaling "red flags") suggests additional criteria: specifically, perceptions of efficacy, conservation of time, and connections to consequences. Regarding the last point, we again call attention to the NASA JPL contract, which specifies two concrete "consequences" for highly rated performance. Specifically, the contract (1) allows awards of $500 million or $1 million per year in flexible funding for performance ratings of "B" or "A," respectively, and (2) provides for option years, contingent on performance at high levels.[244] In that case, the contract was set up with those types of incentives in mind and then built into the structure. An organization would need to be clear on what it wants from the contract, know how to describe it, and know how to grade it to evoke the right behavior; however, many organizations are not yet ready and the evidence on efficacy and efficiency is not unequivocal.[245] Moreover, recalling the NASA JPL contract's caution against grade inflation, neither the financial awards nor option years should be construed as absolute certainties, absent above-average performance. But consequences can take other forms, both positive and negative, including public recognition and remedial action to redirect behavior.

---

[243] Neely, Adams, and Kennerley, 2002.

[244] NASA JPL, 2018b; NASA, 2018a, pp. 18–21.

[245] Stecher et al., 2010, speaks to organizational readiness.

Bibliography

Acosta, Joie D., Rajeev Ramchand, Amariah Becker, Alexandria Felton, and Aaron Kofner, *RAND Suicide Prevention Program Evaluation Toolkit*, Santa Monica, Calif.: RAND Corporation, TL-111-OSD, 2013. As of May 13, 2021:
https://www.rand.org/pubs/tools/TL111.html

Adegbile, Abiodun, David Sarpong, and Dirk Meissner, "Strategic Foresight for Innovation Management: A Review and Research Agenda," *International Journal of Innovation and Technology Management*, Vol. 14, No. 4, August 2017.

Adler, Seymour, Michael Campion, Alan Colquitt, Amy Grubb, Kevin Murphy, Rob Ollander-Krane, and Elaine D. Pulakos, "Getting Rid of Performance Ratings: Genius or Folly? A Debate," *Industrial and Organizational Psychology*, Vol. 9, No. 2, 2016, pp. 219–252.

Aguinis, Herman, "An Expanded View of Performance Management," in James W. Smither and Manuel London, eds., *Performance Management: Putting Research into Action*, San Francisco, Calif.: Jossey-Bass, 2009, pp. 1–44.

———, *Performance Management*, 3rd ed., Boston, Mass.: Pearson Education, 2013.

Aguinis, Herman, Ryan K. Gottfredson, and Harry Joo, "Delivering Effective Performance Feedback: The Strengths-Based Approach," *Business Horizons*, Vol. 55, No. 2, March–April 2012, pp. 105–111.

Allas, Tera, Martin Checinski, Roland Dillon, Richard Dobbs, Andres Cadena, Eoin Daly, David Fine, Solveigh Hieronimus, Navjot Singh, and John Hatwell, *Delivering for Citizens: How to Triple the Success Rate of Government Transformations*, New York: McKinsey, June 2018.

Army Techniques Publication 5-19, *Risk Management*, Washington, D.C.: Headquarters, Department of the Army, April 2014.

Arndt, Craig M., "Using Industry Best Practices to Improve Acquisition," Defense Acquisition University, June 20, 2018. As of May 14, 2021:
https://www.dau.edu/library/defense-atl/blog/Using-Industry-Best-Practices--to-Improve-Acquisition

Atkinson, Anthony A., John H. Waterhouse, and Robert B. Wells, "A Stakeholder Approach to Strategic Performance Measurement," *Sloan Management Review*, Vol. 38, No. 3, 1997, pp. 25–37.

Behn, Robert D., "Why Measure Performance? Different Purposes Require Different Measures," *Public Administration Review*, Vol. 63, No. 5, September 2003, pp. 586–606.

Bell, James B., "Contracting for Evaluation Products and Services," in Joseph S. Wholey, Harry P. Hatry, and Kathryn E. Newcomer, eds., *Handbook of Practical Program Evaluation*, 3rd ed., San Francisco, Calif.: Jossey-Bass, 2010, pp. 620–650.

Bourne, Mike, Andy Neely, John Mills, and Ken Platts, "Implementing Performance Measurement Systems: A Literature Review," *International Journal of Business Performance Management*, Vol. 5, No. 1, 2003a, pp. 1–24.

———, "Why Some Performance Measurement Initiatives Fail: Lessons from the Change Management Literature," *International Journal of Business Performance Management*, Vol. 5, No. 2–3, 2003b, pp. 245–269.

Brown, Trevor L., Matthew Potoski, and David M. Van Slyke, "Managing Public Service Contracts: Aligning Values, Institutions, and Markets," *Public Administration Review*, May–June 2006, pp. 323–331.

———, *Complex Contracting: Government Purchasing in the Wake of the US Coast Guard's Deepwater Program*, New York: Cambridge University Press, 2013.

Bryson, John M., and Michael Q. Patton, "Analyzing and Engaging Stakeholders," in Joseph S. Wholey, Harry P. Hatry, and Kathryn E. Newcomer, eds., *Handbook of Practical Program Evaluation*, 3rd ed., San Francisco, Calif.: Jossey-Bass, 2010, pp. 30–54.

Buckingham, Marcus, and Ashley Goodall, "Reinventing Performance Management," *Harvard Business Review*, April 2015, pp. 40–50.

Cappelli, Peter, and Anna Tavis, "The Performance Management Revolution," *Harvard Business Review*, October 2016, pp. 58–67.

Centers for Disease Control and Prevention, "The National Academies Evaluation of NIOSH Programs," webpage, last reviewed March 26, 2018. As of April 17, 2019: https://www.cdc.gov/niosh/nas/

Cheney, George, Lars Thøger Christensen, Theodore E. Zorn, Jr., and Shiv Ganesh, *Organizational Communication in an Age of Globalization: Issues, Reflections, Practices*, 2nd ed., Long Grove, Ill.: Waveland Press, 2011.

CPARS—*See* Contractor Performance Assessment Reporting System.

Contractor Performance Assessment Reporting System, "Guidance for the Contractor Performance Assessment Reporting System (CPARS)," July 2018.

Davis, Robert C., *Selected International Best Practices in Police Performance Measurement*, Santa Monica, Calif.: RAND Corporation, TR-1153-MOI, 2012. As of May 18, 2021: https://www.rand.org/pubs/technical_reports/TR1153.html

Defense Acquisition University, "Federally Funded Research and Development Centers (FFRDC) and University Affiliated Research Centers (UARCs)," undated a. As of May 18, 2021:
https://www.dau.edu/cop/contracting/DAU%20Sponsored%20Documents/Federally%20Funded%20Research%20and%20Development%20Centers%20(FFRDC)%20and%20University%20Affiliated%20Research%20Centers.pdf

———, "Incentives – Motivating Achievement of Desired Product Support Outcomes," undated b. As of May 11, 2019:
https://www.dau.mil/acquipedia/pages/articledetails.aspx#!521

Demartini, Chiara, *Performance Management Systems: Design, Diagnosis and Use*, Heidelberg, Germany: Physica-Verlag, 2014.

DeNisi, Angelo S., and Kevin R. Murphy, "Performance Appraisal and Performance Management: 100 Years of Progress?" *Journal of Applied Psychology*, Vol. 102, No. 3, 2017, pp. 421–433.

Department of Defense Instruction 5000.77, *DOD Federally Funded Research and Development Center (FFRDC) Program*, Washington, D.C.: U.S. Department of Defense, January 31, 2018.

DoDI—*See* Department of Defense Instruction.

DOE—*See* U.S. Department of Energy.

Doran, George T., "There's a S.M.A.R.T. Way to Write Management's Goals and Objectives," *Management Review*, Vol. 70, No. 11, November 1981, pp. 35–36.

Eisenhardt, Kathleen M., "Building Theories from Case Study Research," *Academy of Management Review*, Vol. 14, No. 4, October 1989, pp. 532–550.

Ferreira, Aldónio, and David Otley, "The Design and Use of Performance Management Systems: An Extended Framework for Analysis," *Management Accounting Research*, Vol. 20, No. 4, December 2009, pp. 263–282.

Gallo, Marcy E., *Federally Funded Research and Development Centers (FFRDCs): Background and Issues for Congress*, Washington, D.C.: Congressional Research Service, R44629, December 1, 2017.

GAO—*See* U.S. Government Accountability Office.

General Services Administration, *Knowledge Worker Productivity: Challenges, Issues, Solutions*, Washington, D.C., June 2011. As of March 28, 2019:
https://www.gsa.gov/cdnstatic/KnowledgeWorkerProductivity.pdf

Gómez-Mejía, Luis R., David B. Balkin, and Robert L. Cardy, *Managing Human Resources*, Englewood Cliffs, N.J.: Prentice Hall, 1995.

Grant, Robert M., *Contemporary Strategy Analysis*, 8th ed., West Sussex, United Kingdom: Wiley, 2013.

Greenfield, Victoria A., Shoshana R. Shelton, and Edward Balkovich, *The Role of Logic Modeling in a Collaborative and Iterative Research Process: Lessons from Research and Analysis Conducted with the Federal Voting Assistance Program*, Santa Monica, Calif.: RAND Corporation, RR-882/1-OSD, 2016. As of July 16, 2021: https://www.rand.org/pubs/research_reports/RR882z1.html

Greenfield, Victoria A., Valerie L. Williams, and Elisa Eiseman, *Using Logic Models for Strategic Planning and Evaluation: Application to the National Center for Injury Prevention and Control*, Santa Monica, Calif.: RAND Corporation, TR-370-NCIPC, 2006. As of May 18, 2021: https://www.rand.org/pubs/technical_reports/TR370.html

Grote, Dick, "3 Popular Goal-Setting Techniques Managers Should Avoid," *Harvard Business Review*, January 2, 2017.

Harvard Business Review, *HBR Guide to Performance Management*, Boston, Mass.: Harvard Business Review Press, 2017.

Hatry, Harry P., James R. Fountain, Jr., Jonathan M. Sullivan, and Lorraine Kremer, eds., *Service Efforts and Accomplishments Reporting: Its Time Has Come: An Overview*, Norwalk, Conn.: Governmental Accounting Standards Board of the Financial Accounting Federation, 1990.

Hatry, Harry P., and Kathryn E. Newcomer, "Pitfalls in Evaluations," in Joseph S. Wholey, Harry P. Hatry, and Kathryn E. Newcomer, eds., *Handbook of Practical Program Evaluation*, 3rd ed., San Francisco, Calif.: Jossey-Bass, 2010, pp. 557–580.

IBM, *IBM Emptoris Supplier Lifecycle Management Performance Evaluation Guide*, Version 10.1.1, 2016. As of May 18, 2021: https://www.ibm.com/docs/en/essm/10.1.1?topic=overview-emptoris-suite-1011-download-doc

Institute of Medicine and National Research Council, *Hearing Loss Research at NIOSH: Reviews of Research Programs of the National Institute for Occupational Safety and Health*, Washington, D.C.: National Academies Press, August 29, 2006.

Johansen, Morgen, Taehee Kim, and Ling Zhu, "Managing for Results Differently: Examining Managers' Purposeful Performance Information Use in Public, Nonprofit, and Private

Organizations," *American Review of Public Administration*, Vol. 48, No. 2, February 2018, pp. 133–147.

Kaplan, Robert S., "Strategic Performance Measurement and Management in Nonprofit Organizations," *Nonprofit Management & Leadership*, Vol. 11, No. 3, Spring 2001, pp. 353–370.

Kaplan, Robert S., and David P. Norton, "Using the Balanced Scorecard as a Strategic Management System," *Harvard Business Review*, Vol. 85, No. 7/8, July–August 2007, pp. 150–161.

Keathley-Herring, Heather, and Eileen M. Van Aken, "Systematic Literature Review on the Factors That Affect Performance Measurement System Implementation," *Proceedings of the 2013 Industrial and Systems Engineering Research Conference*, 2013, pp. 837–846.

King, Cynthia L., Douglas Brook, and Timothy D. Hartge, *Effective Communication Practices During Organizational Transformation: A Benchmarking Study of the U.S. Automobile Industry and U.S. Naval Aviation Enterprise*, Monterey, Calif.: Naval Postgraduate School, NPS-CDMR-GM-07-001, July 2007.

Klonek, Florian E., Nale Lehmann-Willenbrock, and Simone Kauffeld, "Dynamics of Resistance to Change: A Sequential Analysis of Change Agents in Action," *Journal of Change Management*, Vol. 14, No. 3, 2014, pp. 334–360.

Kotter, John P., "Leading Change: Why Transformation Efforts Fail," in Joan V. Gallos, ed., *Organization Development*, San Francisco, Calif.: Jossey-Bass, 2006, pp. 239–251.

———, *Leading Change*, Boston, Mass.: Harvard Business Review Press, 2012.

Kotter, John P., and Leonard A. Schlesinger, "Choosing Strategies for Change," *Harvard Business Review*, Vol. 86, No. 7/8, July–August 2008, pp. 130–139.

Landree, Eric, Hirokazu Miyake, and Victoria A. Greenfield, *Nanomaterial Safety in the Workplace: Pilot Project for Assessing the Impact of the NIOSH Nanotechnology Research Center*, Santa Monica, Calif.: RAND Corporation, RR-1108-NIOSH, 2015. As of May 24, 2021:
https://www.rand.org/pubs/research_reports/RR1108.html

Landree, Eric, and Richard Silberglitt, *Application of Logic Models to Facilitate DoD Laboratory Technology Transfer*, Santa Monica, Calif.: RAND Corporation, RR-2122-OSD, 2018. As of May 24, 2021:
https://www.rand.org/pubs/research_reports/RR2122.html

Larson, Richard C., and Leni Berliner, "On Evaluating Evaluations," *Policy Sciences*, Vol. 16, No. 2, 1983, pp. 147–163.

Lewis, Laurie K., Amy M. Schmisseur, Keri K. Stephens, and Kathleen E. Weir, "Advice on Communicating During Organizational Change: The Content of Popular Press Books," *Journal of Business Communication*, Vol. 43, No. 2, April 2006, pp. 113–137.

Liket, Kellie C., and Karen Maas, "Nonprofit Organizational Effectiveness: Analysis of Best Practices," *Nonprofit and Voluntary Sector Quarterly*, Vol. 44, No. 2, April 2015, pp. 268–296.

Likierman, Andrew, "The Five Traps of Performance Measurement," *Harvard Business Review*, October 2009.

London, Manuel, and James W. Smither, "Feedback Orientation, Feedback Culture, and the Longitudinal Performance Management Process," *Human Resource Management Review*, Vol. 12, No. 1, Spring 2002, pp. 81–100.

Lussier, Robert N., and John R. Hendon, *Human Resource Management: Functions, Applications, and Skill Development*, 3rd ed., Thousand Oaks, Calif.: SAGE Publications, 2019.

Marr, Bernard, *Strategic Performance Management: Leveraging and Measuring Your Intangible Value Drivers*, Burlington, Mass.: Butterworth Heinemann, 2006.

Martinson, Karin, and Carolyn O'Brien, "Conducting Case Studies," in Joseph S. Wholey, Harry P. Hatry, and Kathryn E. Newcomer, eds., *Handbook of Practical Program Evaluation*, 3rd ed., San Francisco, Calif.: Jossey-Bass, 2010, pp. 163–181.

McLaughlin, John A., "Managing for Results, Reaching for Success: A New Paradigm for Planning and Evaluating PT3 Programs," PT3 Grantee Communications Center, U.S. Department of Education, 2001.

———, "An Introduction to Planning, Conducting, and Managing Your Program Evaluation," presentation to the U.S. Environmental Protection Agency, Pathogen Equivalency Committee, September 30, 2003.

Micheli, Pietro, and Jean-Francois Manzoni, "Strategic Performance Measurement: Benefits, Limitations and Paradoxes," *Long Range Planning*, Vol. 43, No. 4, August 2010, pp. 465–476.

Mondy, R. Wayne, *Human Resource Management*, in collaboration with Judy Bandy Mondy, 12th ed., Boston, Mass.: Prentice Hall, 2011.

Moynihan, Donald P., *The Dynamics of Performance Management: Constructing Information and Reform*, Washington, D.C.: Georgetown University Press, 2008.

Moynihan, Donald P., and Noel Landuyt, "How Do Public Organizations Learn? Bridging Cultural and Structural Perspectives," *Public Administration Review*, Vol. 69, No. 6, November–December 2009, pp. 1097–1105.

Narayanamurti, Venkatesh, Laura Diaz Anadon, Gabriel Chan, and Amitai Y. Bin-Nun, "Securing America's Future: Realizing the Potential of the Department of Energy's National Laboratories," testimony presented before the Senate Appropriations Subcommittee on Energy and Water Development, Washington, D.C., October 28, 2015.

NASA—*See* National Aeronautics and Space Administration.

NASA JPL—*See* National Aeronautics and Space Administration Jet Propulsion Laboratory.

National Academies of Sciences, Engineering, and Medicine, *Reducing the Threat of Improvised Explosive Device Attacks by Restricting Access to Explosive Precursor Chemicals*, Washington, D.C.: National Academies Press, 2018.

National Aeronautics and Space Administration, *FY 2019 Volume of Integrated Performance*, Washington, D.C., 2018. As of May 29, 2019:
https://www.nasa.gov/sites/default/files/atoms/files/nasa_2019_volume_of_integrated_performance.pdf

National Aeronautics and Space Administration Jet Propulsion Laboratory, Contract No. 80NM0018D0004P00002, Appendix 2, "The NASA Management Office Performance Appraisal Process: Performance Evaluation and Measurement Plan/Award Term Plan Preparation Guidance," July 26, 2018a, Not available to the general public.

———, "Performance Evaluation and Measurement Plan/Award Term Plan, Performance Period October 1, 2018–September 30, 2019," signed September 28, 2018b, Not available to the general public.

National Aeronautics and Space Administration, Office of Inspector General, *NASA Should Reconsider the Award Evaluation Process and Contract Type for the Operation of the Jet Propulsion Laboratory*, Report No. IG-09-022-Redacted, September 25, 2009.

National Research Council and Institute of Medicine Committee to Review the NIOSH Respiratory Disease Research Program, "Framework for the Review of Research Programs of the National Institute for Occupational Safety and Health," in *Respiratory Diseases Research at NIOSH: Reviews of Research Programs of the National Institute for Occupational Safety and Health*, Appendix A, Washington, D.C.: National Academies Press, August 10, 2007, pp. 173–216. As of April 17, 2019:
https://www.cdc.gov/niosh/nas/pdfs/Framework081007-508.pdf

National Research Council, *The Measure of STAR: Review of the U.S. Environmental Protection Agency's Science to Achieve Results (STAR) Research Grants Program*, Washington, D.C.: National Academies Press, 2003.

Neal, Judith A., and Cheryl L. Tromley, "From Incremental Change to Retrofit: Creating High-Performance Work Systems," *Academy of Management Executive*, Vol. 9, No. 1, February 1995, pp. 42–54.

Neely, Andrew, Chris Adams, and Mike Kennerley, *The Performance Prism: The Scorecard for Measuring and Managing Business Success*, London: Financial Times Prentice Hall, 2002.

Neely, Andrew, and Mike Bourne, "Why Measurement Initiatives Fail," *Measuring Business Excellence*, Vol. 4, No. 4, December 2000, pp. 3–7.

Newcomer, Kathryn E., Harry P. Hatry, and Joseph S. Wholey, "Planning and Designing Useful Evaluations," in Joseph S. Wholey, Harry P. Hatry, and Kathryn E. Newcomer, eds., *Handbook of Practical Program Evaluation*, 3rd ed., San Francisco, Calif.: Jossey-Bass, 2010, pp. 5–29.

Nichols, Sharon L., and David C. Berliner, *Collateral Damage: How High-Stakes Testing Corrupts America's Schools*, Cambridge, Mass.: Harvard Education Press, 2007.

Nitta, Keith A., Sharon L. Wrobel, Joseph Y. Howard, and Ellen Jimmerson-Eddings, "Leading Change of a School District Reorganization," *Public Performance and Management Review*, Vol. 32, No. 3, 2009, pp. 463–488.

O'Reilly, Charles A., and Michael L. Tushman, "Organizational Ambidexterity: Past, Present, and Future," *Academy of Management Perspectives*, Vol. 27, No. 4, November 2013, pp. 324–338.

Paarlberg, Laurie E., and James L. Perry, "Values Management: Aligning Employee Values and Organization Goals," *American Review of Public Administration*, Vol. 37, No. 4, December 2007, pp. 387–408.

Piderit, Sandy Kristin, "Rethinking Resistance and Recognizing Ambivalence: A Multidimensional View of Attitudes Toward an Organizational Change," *Academy of Management Review*, Vol. 25, No. 4, 2000, pp. 783–794.

Poister, Theodore H., "Performance Measurement: Monitoring Program Outcomes," in Joseph S. Wholey, Harry P. Hatry, and Kathryn E. Newcomer, eds., *Handbook of Practical Program Evaluation*, 3rd ed., San Francisco, Calif.: Jossey-Bass, 2010, pp. 100–124.

Prather, Charles W., "The Dumb Thing About SMART Goals for Innovation," *Research-Technology Management*, Vol. 48, No. 5, 2005, pp. 14–15.

Pulakos, Elaine D., *Performance Management: A Roadmap for Developing, Implementing and Evaluating Performance Management Systems*, Alexandria, Va.: SHRM Foundation, 2004.

Pulakos, Elaine D., and Ryan S. O'Leary, "Why Is Performance Management Broken?" *Industrial and Organizational Psychology*, Vol. 4, No. 2, June 2011, pp. 146–164.

Pun, Kit Fai, and Anthony Sydney White, "A Performance Measurement Paradigm for Integrating Strategy Formulation: A Review of Systems and Frameworks," *International Journal of Management Reviews*, Vol. 7, No. 1, March 2005, pp. 49–71.

RAND Corporation, "Forecasting Methodology," webpage, undated. As of April 17, 2019: https://www.rand.org/topics/forecasting-methodology.html

Reeves, Martin, and Jack Fuller, "When SMART Goals Are Not So Smart," *MIT Sloan Management Review*, March 21, 2018.

Riposo, Jessie, Guy Weichenberg, Chelsea Kaihoi Duran, Bernard Fox, William Shelton, and Andreas Thorsen, *Improving Air Force Enterprise Resource Planning-Enabled Business Transformation*, Santa Monica, Calif.: RAND Corporation, RR-250-AF, 2013. As of May 26, 2021: https://www.rand.org/pubs/research_reports/RR250.html

Rogers, Patricia J., and Delwyn Goodrick, "Qualitative Data Analysis," in Joseph S. Wholey, Harry P. Hatry, and Kathryn E. Newcomer, eds., *Handbook of Practical Program Evaluation*, 3rd ed., San Francisco, Calif.: Jossey-Bass, 2010, pp. 429–453.

Rossi, Peter H., Howard E. Freeman, and Mark W. Lipsey, *Evaluation: A Systematic Approach*, 6th ed., Thousand Oaks, Calif.: SAGE Publications, 1999.

Ruegg, Rosalie, and Irwin Feller, *A Toolkit for Evaluating Public R&D Investment: Models, Methods, and Findings from ATP's First Decade*, Gaithersburg, Md.: U.S. Department of Commerce, Technology Administration, National Institute of Standards and Technology, July 2003.

Ruegg, Rosalie, and Gretchen Jordan, *Overview of Evaluation Methods for R&D Programs: A Directory of Evaluation Methods Relevant to Technology Development Programs*, Washington, D.C.: U.S. Department of Energy, Office of Energy Efficiency and Renewable Energy, March 2007.

Schiemann, William A., "Aligning Performance Management with Organizational Strategy, Values, and Goals," in James W. Smither and Manuel London, eds., *Performance Management: Putting Research into Action*, San Francisco, Calif.: Jossey-Bass, 2009, pp. 45–88.

Schneier, Craig Eric, Douglas G. Shaw, and Richard W. Beatty, "Performance Measurement and Management: A Tool for Strategy Execution," *Human Resource Management*, Vol. 30, No. 3, Fall 1991, pp. 279–301.

Scott, Susanne G., and Walter O. Einstein, "Strategic Performance Appraisal in Team-Based Organizations: One Size Does Not Fit All," *Academy of Management Executive*, Vol. 15, No. 2, 2001, pp. 107–116.

Scriven, Michael, and Chris L. S. Coryn, "The Logic of Research Evaluation," *New Directions for Evaluation*, Vol. 2008, No. 118, Summer 2008, pp. 89–105.

Selviaridis, Kostas, and Finn Wynstra, "Performance-Based Contracting: A Literature Review and Future Research Directions," *International Journal of Production Research*, Vol. 53, No. 12, June 2015, pp. 3505–3540.

Silverman, Stanley B., and Wendy M. Muller, "Assessing Performance Management Programs and Policies," in James W. Smither and Manuel London, eds., *Performance Management: Putting Research into Action*, San Francisco, Calif.: Jossey-Bass, 2009, pp. 527–554.

Smith, Keith, "Measuring Innovation," in Jan Fagerberg, David C. Mowery, and Richard R. Nelson, eds., *The Oxford Handbook of Innovation*, Oxford, United Kingdom: Oxford University Press, 2005, pp. 148–179.

Smither, James W., and Manuel London, eds., *Performance Management: Putting Research into Action*, San Francisco, Calif.: Jossey-Bass, 2009.

Stecher, Brian M., Frank Camm, Cheryl L. Damberg, Laura S. Hamilton, Kathleen J. Mullen, Christopher Nelson, Paul Sorensen, Martin Wachs, Allison Yoh, Gail L. Zellman, and Kristin J. Leuschner, *Toward a Culture of Consequences: Performance-Based Accountability Systems for Public Services*, Santa Monica, Calif.: RAND Corporation, MG-1019, 2010. As of May 26, 2021:
https://www.rand.org/pubs/monographs/MG1019.html

Steiss, Alan W., *Strategic Management for Public and Nonprofit Organizations*, New York: Marcel Dekker, 2003.

Torraco, Richard J., "Writing Integrative Literature Reviews: Using the Past and Present to Explore the Future," *Human Resource Development Review*, Vol. 15, No. 4, December 2016, pp. 404–428.

U.S. Army Environmental Command, *Environmental Program Internal Assessment Guide*, Version 1.0, March 27, 2013.

U.S. Code, Title 10, Section 2304, "Contracts: Competition Requirements," January 3, 2012.

U.S. Department of Energy and Ames Laboratory, "Performance Evaluation Measurement Plan (PEMP), Applicable to the Operation of Ames Laboratory," Contract No. DE-AC02-07CH11358, 2018.

U.S. Department of Energy, Office of Science, "Office of Science Lab Appraisal Process," webpage, undated. As of June 3, 2021:
https://www.energy.gov/science/office-science-lab-appraisal-process

U.S. Department of Homeland Security Risk Steering Committee, "DHS Risk Lexicon: 2010 Edition," September 2010. As of April 2, 2019:
https://www.dhs.gov/xlibrary/assets/dhs-risk-lexicon-2010.pdf

U.S. Government Accountability Office, "NASA Procurement: Use of Award Fees for Achieving Program Outcomes Should Be Improved," Washington, D.C., GAO-07-58, January 2007.

———, "Performance Measurement and Evaluation: Definitions and Relationships," Washington, D.C., GAO-11-646SP, May 2011. As of June 3, 2021:
https://www.gao.gov/products/gao-11-646sp

———, *National Laboratories: DOE Needs to Improve Oversight of Work Performed for Non-DOE Entities*, Washington, D.C., GAO-14-78, October 2013.

———, *Department of Energy: Performance Evaluations Could Better Assess Management and Operating Contractor Costs*, Washington, D.C., GAO-19-5, February 2019.

Van Dooren, Wouter, Geert Bouckaert, and John Halligan, *Performance Management in the Public Sector*, New York: Routledge, 2010.

Weiss, Carol H., *Evaluation Research: Methods of Assessing Program Effectiveness*, Englewood Cliffs, N.J.: Prentice-Hall, 1973.

Wholey, Joseph S, "Use of Evaluation in Government: The Politics of Evaluation," in Joseph S. Wholey, Harry P. Hatry, and Kathryn E. Newcomer, eds., *Handbook of Practical Program Evaluation*, 3rd ed., San Francisco, Calif.: Jossey-Bass, 2010, pp. 651–667.

Williams, Valerie L., Elisa Eiseman, Eric Landree, and David M. Adamson, *Demonstrating and Communicating Research Impact: Preparing NIOSH Programs for External Review*, Santa Monica, Calif.: RAND Corporation, MG-809-NIOSH, 2009. As of June 4, 2021:
https://www.rand.org/pubs/monographs/MG809.html

W.K. Kellogg Foundation, *The Step-by-Step Guide to Evaluation: How to Become Savvy Evaluation Consumers*, Battle Creek, Mich., 2017.